RETREAT TO VICTORY
IN 1915

by
Nancy J. Cramer

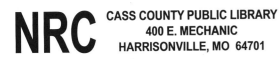

SYNOPSIS OF BOOK:

Approximately one-half of the 220,000 Serbian Soldiers who fought the Austrians in 1914, then the Germans and Bulgarians in 1915, miraculously survived the hardships and rigors of walking as many as 400 miles to cross the Albanian mountains. They crossed the treacherous ice and snow-covered mountains to reach the Adriatic coastline, where Allied ships waited to take them to regain their health in the safety of the Greek island of Corfu. They reorganized as an army and went to Salonika, where with the French and the British, they defeated the Bulgarians. This campaign ultimately led to the Bulgarians surrendering to the Serbs and their Allies. Serbia belonged to the Serbs now.

Most Serbians returned to what was left of their homes and families and began a new life. It was not the old life, but an entirely new one. At last, Serbia's dream came true. After nearly six hundred years of Ottoman occupation, the "Republic of Serbia, the Croats and Slovenes" became a reality by the Treaty of Versailles, signed in Paris on June 28, 1919.

"The road was a moving mass of transport of all kinds—motor-wagons, bullock-wagons, horse-wagons, men and guns…all intent on escape. This procession has been passing continuously for days, stretching from one end of Serbia to the other. It was the passing of a whole nation into exile, a people leaving a lost country."

William Smith, Scottish Women's Hospital, November 15, 1915.
Courtesy National World War I Museum and Memorial,
Kansas City, Missouri, USA.

Front Cover: Drawing by Vivian Kallmann.

ISBN – 978-0-9857603-4-2

Printed by Walsworth Publishing Company, Inc. Marceline MO.
Dennis Paalhar, Sales Representative

A portion of the proceeds from *Retreat to Victory* will go to the Save the Serbian Children organization.

Map of Serbia in 1914 – *Public Domain*

CONTENTS

PART ONE

BRIEF HISTORY OF SERBIA AND THE BALKANS

PART TWO

START OF THE WAR

PART THREE

SERBIAS' DEFENSE

THIS BOOK IS DEDICATED

*to the Serbs who lived through this ordeal, to those who died,
and to those who lived on as-if they had died.*

*Suffering existed for the people of the former Kingdom of Serbia. Suffering beyond
imagination from all the ills of mankind---starvation, freezing, fear of the known and
the unknown, helplessness, and most of all, hopelessness. Serbia would be reduced to a
country without people, property or dignity.*

*In one Serbian town, a plinth supports a square column marking each of the four wars of
the 1800's. The names on the stones tell Serbia's story of the nineteenth century.*

This book tells Serbia's story of 1914-1918.

General (Voyoda) Putnik is carried in an enclosed chair through the Retreat because of his ill health. The four soldiers rotate with others every 45 or so minutes because of the weight of their burden and the difficult route they traveled. *Drawing of Putnik being carried in chair – by Vivian Kallmann.*

This monument was built on the median strip of one of the few four lane highways in Serbia near a small town. Note the number of men from that area who died in the three wars Serbia fought in 1912, 1913, and 1914-18. It is estimated that up to 56% of the male population was decimated by war, and more, if all ages of males were included. *Photo by Nancy Cramer.*

ACKNOWLEDGEMENTS

First and foremost, I thank my faithful guide and interpreter, Branko Bosilikov, whose skill and perspicuity in finding the right people to interview, as well as satisfactory hotels and restaurants, was vital. Without his aid, there would have been no book. We have continued our friendship via the internet, and he occasionally corrects my unintelligible notes.

Next to receive praise is Father Aleksander Bugarin, parish priest of St. George's Orthodox Church, Lenexa, Kansas, whose skills at translation were invaluable. A native of Montenegro and the son of a priest, he told about the ceremonies and important religious figures as well as traditions of the time. His support and kindness were inspiring, and the many lists of Serbian-American organizations and churches he provided were helpful.

The assistance given by several people in translations also include Mr. Vladimir Rokvic of Chicago, who translated and added information to a series of pictures from various national, state and city archives. Unfortunately, space prohibited the use of many of these. Also Ms. Mira Stevovichilich and Father Radomir Chkautovich were most helpful also in providing lyrics to the famous poem, "The Blue Sea Graveyard." They also helped me with the spelling of the different towns and sites in Serbia. I have used the spelling of names as they were written in the 1914 time period.

Two local men encouraged me with their story . They were Lazar Jovanovic, son of a young boy survivor, and Milo Colek, grandnephew of that same survivor. When I discovered their residence in the Kansas City area, I knew this was a book I was meant to write. It was destiny. We visited a number of times, and Mr. Jovanovic showed me the certificate his father received certifying him as a survivor of the Retreat. Milo and I met with Jonathan Casey, Director of Archives and the Edward Jones Research Center at the National World War I Museum and Memorial, to discuss a possible exhibit on Serbia. That has yet to come to fruition.

Jonathan was most helpful in providing me with archival photos and information and the full use of the Research Center and its facilities. Stacie Peterson, registrar, promptly provided what I needed. Thanks to both of you, and to Doran Cart, Senior Curator, for his extensive knowledge of uniforms, guns, rifles and odd things you never saw before.

In Serbia, I met Bosilijka Stevanovic, a guide, who furnished me several stories and photographs of relatives who served in the Retreat. Her additions were most helpful, as were those made by Ljubomir Saramandic, curator of the Corfu Museum. The museum, though small, has excellent collections which document the stay and recuperation of the Serbians, as well as the work of the government during 1916-1918. Mr. Saramandic has written his own version of the Corfu experience and had it translated into English.

Not to be overlooked is Mr. Fraser Simm, archivist at Heriot's School in Edinburgh, Scotland, who prepared papers and photos for my examination and photographing during my visit to the school. He told me about the daily routine of the students and the history of the school. Coincidently, I also met American members of the Heriot family who were visiting there that weekend. There is a Heriot Family Association in the United States. Also a visitor at that time was Ms. Louise Miller, a resident of Edinburgh, who shared her continued research into the lives of the boys at Heriot, which added much to my story. She also recommended the book, *The Snows of Serbia, A Child Soldier in the Great War*. I am grateful to Flora Brown, for her expertise assistance in editing, and to Carla Grant, whose computer knowledge saved me valuable time in formatting and preparing the manuscript for the publisher. Thanks, ladies.

Other people, once they heard of my project, called or e-mailed items of information, but unfortunately, over the passage of time, some of those notes have been mislaid. You know who you are, so please accept my thanks now.

My artist, Vivian Kallmann, contributed her talent to an earlier published book, *Beko, the little French Dog*. She and I work on the same wave length, and it was a joy to have her do the drawings for this book also. Thanks so much, Vivian.

Last of all, to my dear friend and fellow writer, Niel Johnson, whose patience and encouragement kept me going when "the going was tough." His extraordinary knowledge of history (even Serbian) and excellent vocabulary filled in my many gaps. As you can surmise from his commentary, his rapid assimilation of Serbia's history speaks for itself. Thank you, Mr. President (he impersonates President Truman). He valiantly edited the several sets of book proofs

And most of all, I am grateful to the Serbian people, whose courage and fortitude created one of the greatest stories of suffering and determination the world has ever experienced.

The photos marked with three asterisks are from a 1915-1916 album in various archives in Beograd. My appreciation to those authors who 100 years ago assembled these magnificent photographs of the war, the Retreat, and the fighting in Salonika. All photos are in the Public Domain, thanks to Serbian rules for usage, unless otherwise credited.

Mausoleum on Vido Island in memory of the Serbian dead. *Public Domain****.

WHY I WROTE THIS BOOK:

It was on my first trip in 2012 to Serbia of three that I heard the story of the 20,000 boys ages 12 to 16, who were conscripted by the Serbian army in 1914 to save them from their enemies, the Central Powers. Of this number, only about 5,000 are believed to have survived a long and dangerous retreat. Then I read about Retreat of the soldiers, besieged by the enemy at their rear. Accompanying the soldiers were thousands of peasants, fearful of the brutal retribution from the Austrians and especially the Bulgarians, their historic enemy.

The Serbs formed four routes of retreat through the Morava Valley and across the Albanian Mountains to the Adriatic Sea, where in 1915-1916 Allied ships waited to rescue the boys, soldiers and civilians. Many of the 5,000 surviving boys were sent to France and England and other countries to be housed and educated. I visited one of those schools, Heriot School, in Edinburgh, Scotland. I have use school records, old letters, and many emails from Serbian-Americans to construct their historic story.

This story is seen through the eyes of an anonymous Soldier, who represents all the 450,000 Serbian troops. He sees them fighting, marching, resting, and dying, but he makes no response. He is the soul of Serbia.

The book ends with the surviving Serbians fighting the Bulgarians, leading to the surrender of Bulgaria in October 1918. Germany signed the Armistice the next month, ending the carnage and devastation of World War I. The Serbian story is almost completely unknown in the United States. Hopefully, this book about the Serbian peoples' incredible courage and patriotism, will fill that void.

Note: Wherever possible I have used the old spellings of names, rivers and cities. Some noted historians disagree about the use of "Austro-Hungary" and "Austria-Hungary." I chose the latter because it is more familiar to the reader. The same way I used the modern spelling of "Belgrade" rather than the Serbian "Belgrad."

This is a peasant's wagon; most had a cloth cover to protect the passengers and household goods they carried. Usually, all family members walked except the very young and very old. They walked as much as 400 miles in the Retreat. It sits on the grounds of the Belgrade Fort in Belgrade. *Photo of the wagon by Nancy Cramer.*

1

BRIEF HISTORY OF SERBIA AND THE BALKANS

WHAT PRICE MUST BE PAID FOR FREEDOM?

The suffering of the Serbs is hard to imagine. There was the fear of the known and unknown difficulties that surely lay ahead. Almost insoluble problems faced the thousands of Serbs of all ages who made or attempted to make the treacherous crossing of the Albanian mountains in 1915. Feelings of hopelessness and helplessness described the nearly half a million Serbian soldiers and civilians in that winter of 1915. The advancing, menacing armies of the Central Powers were determined to drain the life blood out of Serbia and reduce her to a country devoid of all that constitutes a nation. But to the world's astonishment, as reported by a few courageous American and British correspondents and photographers accompanying the Retreat, most of the people never considered giving up their quest.

It all began with a shot. A pistol shot, then another one that took the lives of the Archduke of Austria-Hungary and his wife on June 28, 1914. Then more shots came a month later from Austrian gunboats sailing down the Sava River to attack Belgrade, Serbia's capital, located on a cape of land bound by rivers on each side, the Sava and the Danube. The attack and subsequent fighting over the next four months surprised the European world because the Serbians emerged victorious. After a few months of futility, Austria withdrew her armies. They would return the next year with the might of the German army and its huge unmatchable artillery. The Bulgarians were also persuaded later to join the fight against the Serbs in revenge for their defeat in the previous Balkan War of 1913.

Tradition has it that Serbians were born to be fighters, but they knew their victory would not last. They used the interim to bolster the size of their small army to almost 450,000 men of all ages. They conscripted the old men who formed the Third Ban. The *cheechas* or "Uncles" came with no uniforms and old Turkish muskets in answer to their nation's appeal. The government pleaded with the French and British for help in replacing their old Turkish muskets. Some modern rifles did come through, but only about a third of what was needed. More importantly, the artillery sent was almost negligible in numbers.

Worse yet, some of the cartridges and shells were of the wrong bore, and the machinery at Kragujevatz, Serbia's main manufacturing armament plant, had to re-bore the weapons' barrels. One reason the Allies could not supply more was that they had a desperate need for more weapons themselves to fight the battles on the Western Front. The other problem, equally hard to resolve, was the lack of modern transportation to Serbia. It had only one railroad which ran north and south with limited mileage.

The ruler, King Petar Karadjordevic, was a 70-year-old seasoned veteran of various wars who had fought for freedom from the Ottoman Turks several times. A monument in a town square commemorates the wars of 1804, 1815, 1848, and 1877 with inscriptions on each side. Some of the *chetniks* (or irregulars) fought alongside the regular army in the latter wars. (In post-World War II the chetniks earned a dubious reputation while performing guerilla acts against the Tito regime.) Gradually, Serbia gained a degree of independence from the Ottomans with each war, and the Balkan Wars of 1912 and 1913 added the final independence they had fought centuries to obtain. However, at the same time, the victories increased the enmity of her victims, chiefly Albanians to the west and Bulgarians to the east. This relationship with Bulgaria had been contentious for centuries, but the Serbians, ever hopeful, continued their quest for restoring their borders of an earlier age.

From their blood will spring flowers
For some faroff generation.
by Njegos

From book by Olive M. Aldridge,
The Retreat from Serbia through Montenegro and Albania

THE SOLDIER

The Soldier represents each Serbian soldier. He is a young man and untried; he is also mature and experienced at soldiering; and finally, he represents an old man who has fought, and is weary with aching bones, but his belly contains enough fire yet to make him fight for a Greater Serbia. It is through the eyes of The Soldier that we see the struggle and trauma of the Retreat. It is from his thoughts that we understand the unrelenting demands the Retreat required.

And it is through his feelings, though seldom expressed, that we enter the heart of the Serbians as they seek to find their individual destiny, be it life or death.

ABOVE: These skulls are part of the Skull Tower built to commemorate the sacrifice by the Serbian soldiers in the battle with the Ottoman Turks in 1813. (See next page for the story) *Photo by Nancy Cramer.*

RIGHT: This statue shows soldiers fighting for and obtaining piece by piece their independence from the Ottoman Empire in four wars that occurred in the 1800's. *Photo by Nancy Cramer.*

PART TWO

START OF THE WAR

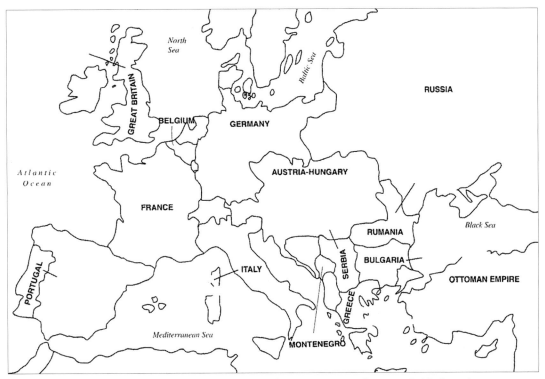

This map shows tiny Serbia just below Austria-Hungary, her enemy. *Map of Europe – Public Domain.*

SERBIA'S TROUBLED HISTORY

Serbia's efforts to become an independent nation extend back to the 800's when the country was first formed as part of the Byzantine Empire. Its geographical location provided access south to Greece and the Mediterranean and east to the Black Sea. Because of these desirable routes, the vulnerable country was constantly harassed or attacked by other countries seeking the access. In the time honored battle with the Ottoman Turks at the famous "Kosovo Polje" or "Field of the Blackbirds" in 1389, Serbia lost its hard-won independence and some territory. Thereafter, the small country staged numerous uprisings and battles against Ottoman overlords in the centuries that followed. The Kingdom of Serbia in different time periods was a vast country. It had included Bosnia-Herzegovina, Croatia, Montenegro, Albania, and parts of Roumania, Macedonia, Kosovo, and northern Greece.

The Serbs engaged in several major wars in the 1800's. The Serbo-Turkish war of 1876-1878 was fought by Serbia and Montenegro to support uprisings in neighboring Bosnia and Herzegovina. This war only deepened the Balkan crisis that led to the Russo-Turkish War of 1877-1878. However, the result was independence for Serbia and

Montenegro from the Ottoman Empire as well as an increase in their territory. The war began when Christian peasants in Herzegovina rebelled against the Muslim landlords and Ottoman Turkish rulers. The revolt spread to Bosnia. These results were formalized in an agreement by the major powers at the Berlin Congress in 1878. Another war, the Serbo-Bulgarian, was settled in 1886, uniting Bulgaria and Rumelia, while re-establishing the prewar borders of Serbia and Bulgaria.

The year 1908 provided what could be considered as provocation for the start of World War I when Austria-Hungary formally annexed Bosnia and Herzegovina. The Serbians had viewed these countries as part of what they expected was to become Greater Serbia. Angry at the action, the Serbs mobilized, preparing to fight for those two countries. However, Europe became alarmed and Germany pressured Russia to convince their "Slavic brothers," as the Serbs were named, to de-mobilize and accept the annexation. Thereafter, Belgrade maintained a cautious attitude in its official relations with Vienna.

Serbia, chafing under the pressure from Russia, still held the goal of obtaining the freedom of Kosovo, Macedonia, and other regions from Ottoman rule. As a result, they commenced the First Balkan War of 1912. Bulgaria and Greece joined Serbia and Montenegro in invading Macedonia and the European part of Turkey to overthrow the Ottomans. They were successful, and Turkey was reduced to a small area centered around Constantinople. The Bulgarians had previously won their release from the Ottomans and joined in the fighting, hoping to gain more territory.

However, the next year, 1913, in the Second Balkan War, Bulgaria attacked her former allies in a failed attempt to regain territory she had originally been promised to receive. This deepened the enmity between the two major Balkan countries, Serbia and Bulgaria. The European powers, especially Austria-Hungary, became alarmed. Meanwhile, Serbia gained control of Kosovo.

King Petar Assumes Power

During this decade of wars, the Serbian military in 1903 murdered the unpopular Serbian King Aleksander along with his equally disliked wife. The man who became the new king, Petar Karadjordevic, had been in exile and was aware of the plot and the terrible reign of Aleksander. He returned to Serbia and righted many of the wrongs the previous monarch had enacted. Among these acts were restoring and liberalizing the constitution; setting the country's finances in order; and improving trade and education. Making schools available to more children was essential, as 80% of the population was illiterate.

Although these actions by King Petar found favor with his countrymen, it was his role as monarch during the ensuing Retreat of 1915-1916 and afterwards, that earned him even more respect. Previously, in a harsh punitive reaction to King Petar assuming the throne, Austria in 1905 placed a punitive tariff on imports of livestock, mostly pigs, which were Serbia's main export. King Petar, instead of retaliating, sought other trade routes and an outlet to the seas, chiefly by threatening to seize control of Albania. It was this latter action, however, that the major powers rejected. In 1913, Serbia was forced to give up all claims to Albanian land. As a result of the 1913 war, many brutal acts were committed by both Serbia and Albania. These barbaric deeds made it more dangerous for the Serbians when they had to cross the Albanian mountains in their subsequent Retreat of 1915. Retaliation was swift and cruel by Albanian mountaineers.

The bloody history of the Balkans with its ethnic rivalries, its different religions, the language barriers, and cultural differences continued through World War I with Bulgaria perpetuating obscene barbarities on its neighbors, Macedonia, Kosovo and Serbia. Bulgaria, after the Austrian-Hungarian invasion of Serbia, decided late in the war to join the Central Powers and punish Serbia, and try to regain the lost land it sought. The Tower of Skulls from the war of 1809 in Nis* was duplicated in 1915 in numerous places, only one of numerous acts of barbarism that scarred the villages of Serbia and its neighbors.

For a few years after World War I ended, the bloodshed lessened to a great extent. However, internal rivalries in the decade before World War II would start the bloody fountain flowing again. That brought Marshall Tito to power in 1945 and the nation of Yugoslavia into being.

(This hideous monument was created in 1813 during the First Serbian Uprising when Turkish army forces attacked the rebel group led by Stevan Sindelic. The Serbs were overwhelmed and rather than face the usual punishment of impalement, Sindelic chose to explode a powder magazine, killing himself, all his men and any nearby Turks. Their heads were recovered and 952 were mounted into a pillar of concrete as a warning to Serbs to stop rebelling. Only 54 skulls remain today but the tower is one of the most gruesome battle sights I have ever seen.)

"As morning dawned upon the Eastern hills,
Two great ravens soared in circles black
Above the spreading plain of Kossovo.
They came to rest upon the tower, white
Save once more our Fatherland,
Our King and patriotic band.
Save once more our Fatherland,
Our King and patriotic band."

This poem refers to the Battle of Kossovo in 1389 on what has been named "The Field of Blackbirds" because the birds were drawn to the huge number of fallen soldiers of both the Serbs and the Ottoman Turks.

· ·

"If, as Burns said, songs make the country, in Serbia 'tis courage makes the songs.'"
(Quote from Elbridge Colby, University of Minnesota,
in *The Sewanee Review*, Vol. 25, No. 1 (Jan. 1917). Johns Hopkins University Press)

AUSTRIA PRESENTS AN ULTIMATUM
A Story as Envisioned by the Author

The Soldier stood guard by the polished oak doors that closed the room to view but could not shut out the loud voices of the authorities as they argued. "This is preposterous, insulting, and totally unacceptable," one Serbian official said. Another agreed with him, pounding his fist on a table. "Now, now," King Petar's moderating voice could be heard between the exclamations of the others. "I am sure if I call the Czar, he will reason with

Wilhelm, who will explain the rashness of Austria's demands." However, it was useless. The shouting and table pounding continued. The Soldier dared not look at the guard opposite him to see his reactions. He knew what they would be. He knew what the reaction would be of all 250,000 Serbian soldiers who had survived the two recent wars in 1912 and 1913 and the typhus epidemic brought under control the past winter.

Serbia would never concede to the ultimatum that had been presented a few hours ago by the ambassador of Austria-Hungary. Moreover, an answer was demanded within 24 hours. The Serbs were outnumbered six to one in soldiers and twelve to one in artillery. It would be a massacre of the Serbs even if the enemy felt the Serbian bayonet in his belly or fell from the well-aimed bullet of experienced Serbian gunners.

Many of the enemy troops were Slavs also, from countries that Austria had taken over completely, such as Czech, Slovak, or Bosnia and Herzegovinia. There were more than twelve different languages or dialects the Austrian officers had to contend with in commanding this diverse army. The Soldier asked himself, "Would they be effective commanders during the fighting? Or would the Serbs have a chance that some Slavic brothers would cross over to our lines? If only Germany stays out, we might have a chance," The Soldier reasoned.

His duty time ended when his replacement came. But as The Soldier left the building, he knew well what the Serbian answer would be to the ultimatum from Austria.

REACTIONS OF NATIONS TO AUSTRIA'S ULTIMATUM

Austria's ultimatum to Serbia, sent on July 23, 1914, generated varying reactions among the major European powers. What Austria had anticipated as a sharp "slap on the wrist" for Serbia to bring her into line with Austria's demands served as a slap in the face for Russia and Germany. The British completely ignored the question temporarily. The Irish question occupied their attention.

The ultimatum contained ten points. The one that was most offensive to Serbia dealt with the investigation of the assassination of the Archduke and his wife. Austria proposed to lead the investigation. In all, the ultimatum also provided openings by which Austria could destroy the independence of Serbia. The Serbian answer was to be presented within 48 hours of the 6 p.m. delivery.

Previously, on July 4, Austria's Count Leopold of Germany's Foreign Office, contemplating such action by Austria, is quoted calmly as saying the German Foreign Office would offer "unconditional support for any course of action Austria chose to adopt." Count Alexander Hoyos, an Austrian diplomat, asserted that Germany would easily win the war against France. The other countries of Western Europe paid little attention to what they called –" the Balkan bickering."

Actually, the general belief was that nothing of importance would be served by another Balkan War, as Europe had its own problems. France was politically unstable, having seven changes of government between 1911 and 1914. Meanwhile, Serbia's Prince Regent Alexander, educated in Russia, asked the Russians for 120,000 rifles. They were promised but never delivered. On the day the ultimatum was delivered, the Russian General Sazonov ordered the mobilization of the Russian army immediately—one hour after the publication of the ultimatum. Some of his soldiers had to travel as far as 700 miles to reach their regiments. Russia ordered repatriation of 100 million rubles of state funds from Berlin, saying it would be an intolerable betrayal to allow Serbia to succumb to an Austrian attack. The Russian army and ministers said they were prepared to fight.

In Germany, the opposite reaction took place when 100,000 Germans all around the country staged a series of protests against going to war. Other examples of political unrest also existed in Germany involved laborers going on strikes. The new politicians were unused to deal with the consequences. Stability among the masses was in doubt until German General Eric von Falkenhayn, chief of the Imperial German General Staff, forced the issue. However, there was no coordination with Austria as to where the German troops were to be sent or where Austrian troops would be stationed. This was particularly crucial for the Austrian troops, as they were poorly trained and had no mountain guns to use in the hilly sections of Serbia.

Consequently, the confusion created by the chaos was vented upon local Austrians with Serbian heritage, with hundreds being arrested and the borders shut down. Fifty men were executed in the city of Dubrovnik, Albania, causing thousands of men of Serbian background to cross unguarded borders to return to serve in the Serbian army. The partisans or *komitadji*, who normally harassed the army soldiers, now fought alongside the Serbs. One-third of the men lacked rifles, so Serb policemen raided the houses to confiscate privately owned guns for the army.

In Britain, the Parliament was so involved with the Ulster (Ireland) crisis that it was not until a few days later on 24 July that the *London Times* acknowledged the "gravity of the situation. We stand on the verge of war."

Serbia quickly mobilized nearly 500,000 men from a population of less than four million. Four-fifths of them were stationed along the western front, near the border with Austria. Many conscripts had no uniforms, only tunics and the highly identifiable Serbian hats, or *sajkaca*. Several gypsies led their units by playing their bagpipes or the gypsy style of fiddle. That is, the gypsies played, until they met the machine guns of the Austrians. The playing stopped because the players were dead.

THE MILITARY STATUS OF THE SERBIAN ARMY

Engaging in the wars of 1912 and 1913, for a small country like Serbia, meant depletion of many resources. At least 36,000 men were casualties; the national treasury was drained; and large numbers of peasant soldiers had not been able to farm. With so many men in the army, the farm labor was supplied by women and older men and young boys. This led to a serious depletion of the food supply with famine in a few places. Whereas, Serbia came out victorious in both wars and regained the land called "Kosovo," so essential to the remaking of her historical past, she paid a tremendous price which would handicap her for the demands of the next few years.

Although the bravery of its soldiers was praised worldwide, Serbia was ranked as the most poorly equipped army in Europe with the exception of tiny Montenegro, her steadfast ally, who ranked lower. For example, there was a shortage of .30 caliber rifles for The Soldiers, and each regiment had only four Maxim machine guns. Ammunition for those machine guns and for modern rifles, along with artillery shells, were in great demand throughout the battlegrounds of Europe. Serbia had only one place of production, the town of Kragujevac. All other types of weapons and ammunition had to be imported. When fighting began in Western Europe in August 1914, the Allies were also in dire need for weapons, so supplying Serbia often came last on their list.

Consequently, the large Western nations and the United States were aghast when the heavily armored gun boat, *Temes*, from the mighty Austrian-Hungarian army, sailed down the Sava River on July 28, 1914, and began shelling Serbia's capital city of Belgrade. This unexpected attack against Belgrade caught Serbia unaware, but the Serbian fighting skills forced the Austrians to depart by December 1914. There was a lull in the fighting which did not last long. In the spring 1915, a combined German and Austrian army force of 20 divisions invaded Serbia. Their armies were joined later by ten Bulgarian divisions and these forces had superior artillery guns. The Germans had recently succeeded in convincing Bulgaria to make a secret pact with the Central Powers. The combined troops forced the Serbians that year to retreat, but not surrender.

Hardened by their long history of having to fight for their freedom, the Serbs displayed the resolve and courage that led to their successful Retreat and rescue by the French and Italians to safety in other lands. By 1916 the Serbians joined their Allies in Greece and defeated the Bulgarians, leading to the end of World War I.

This is their story.

A DESCRIPTION OF SERBIA IN 1914

Serbia was one of the smaller European nations, about the size of America's state of Ohio, or 34,116 square miles. Overall, four-fifths of Serbia is mountainous, with the only fertile land, the Morava Valley, running north and south. In the north the mountains are low, 2,000 to 3,000 feet, but in the south they attain a height of 6,000 to 7,000 feet. The southwestern mountains, which form borders with Albania and Macedonia, rise to great heights of 8,000 feet. These are the mountains the Serbians crossed in the Retreat.

Large rivers separate Serbia into sections: the Danube and Sava in the north; the Drina in the west; the Morava, Kolobara, Drina, and Timok along the plains. These rivers create huge floods in rainy seasons. A large gorge on the border of Serbia and Roumania, "The Iron Gates," also creates a formidable water hazard. The southward running Vardar River connects with the Aegean Sea in the southeast. All of these rivers were scenes of fierce battles in the war.

At the outbreak of the war in 1914, Serbia had a population of about 4.7 million people. As a result of adding more land won by the victories of the Balkan Wars of 1912 and 1913, about 1.7 million people had come under Serbian jurisdiction. The population also now included 160,000 Romanians, a few Turks and Albanians, and 8,000 Austrian-Hungarians. About 47,000 gypsies and 5,000 Jews completed the total population.

The army was comprised of 10 major divisions, each named for the area from which its soldiers came (i.e. Morava, Drina, Danube, Shumadia, Timok, Ibar, Kossovo, Vardar, Bregalnica and Monastir and others.) Recruiting was constantly taking place, and volunteers of Slavic origin who lived in other countries crossed borders to increase the ranks. At least 5,000 Serbian-American citizens came from the United States to fight, as well as Slavs who escaped from other armies throughout Europe. (See story p.142 about American Serbs.)

Transportation of men and supplies was a perennial problem. A national registry was made of all the horses and oxen, and those who drove the animals were exempt from military service. Often, however, these teams hauled artillery and supplies, and if not in the midst of an attack, the oxen and their drivers were on the outskirts of the fighting and still exposed to danger.

The lack of medical military staff reflected the national overall shortage of doctors and nurses. That is one reason the typhus epidemic swept the nation so rapidly. It also resulted in many humanitarian medical foreign personel who flocked to Serbia in sympathy for the Serbs and their great need for medical services. England and the United States were among the leading volunteers, but others came from Australia, Japan, and dozens of other countries. The international response was overwhelming.

Railroad transportation was in terrible conditions. The only north-south line ran from Belgrade to nearby Djevdjelija and from Nis (Nish) to Sofia in Bulgaria. This line was the main branch of transportation. Other small branches with limited capacity extended into the countryside. This was one reason the British and French had so much difficulty getting supplies to the Serbian armies. There was a total of 5,000 miles of roads of various quality. Most were poorly constructed and became rivers of mud in the rainy seasons. Transporting supplies to armies in the fields presented numerous problems, and conservation of ammunition was vital to the Serbian effort.

Overall, Serbia was an agricultural nation, and its people were farmers. There was little industry, which created an enormous problem during the war. Arms and ammunition had to be supplied by the French, English and Russians. The main export had been pigs and wine to Austria, and Austria controlled the pricing to influence the economy of Serbia. Austria and Germany both wanted easier access to the Aegean Sea, and a secure railroad through the Morava Valley would have solved this need.

The Serbians were strongly religious and valued their priests highly. The church, however, it was rumored, kept the best scholars to serve as priests instead of sending them on to European universities. Some wealthy families enrolled their sons in mostly German and English universities. Nevertheless, their war experiences generated a number of men who were to become famous poets and writers. Much of their work is just now being translated into English, so the English speaking literary world is not yet familiar with the beauty of their writing. (Look in the bibliography for suggestions of translated works.)

Serbian prisoners of war. *Public Domain.*

SERBIA'S DEFENSE

THE BATTLE OF FORT BELGRADE
A Story as Envisioned by the Author

The Soldier crouched behind a ragged limestone rock on the mountainside, peering at the Sava River in the distance. Austrian gun boats were rapidly making their way toward the junction with the Danube which flowed from the east. The two rivers met at Belgrade, where the fort on the bluff had protected the city for hundreds of years. The Austrian artillery guns were aimed at the fort and soon fired the first of many salvos. Puffs of smoke from the guns floated upward like small clouds. Firing rapidly, the gun crews lifted shells, shoved, closed the breech block, and pulled the firing cork, almost mechanically as if in one single action.

The guns of the fort responded, some shells hitting the boats, most skipping across the waters, making wavelets and bubbles. Some Austrian gunners sought safety in the bottoms of their boats, but most continued their devilish bombardment. Soon, Serbs on the fort's wall were clutching their bodies, while large chips of rocks flew from the fort's formerly impervious wall. The battle went on for an hour. Serbs opposite the fort hunched

The Fort had protected the city for hundreds of years with its tall, strong walls. Note the artillery of various wars atop the walls and the few openings and gates. *Photo by Nancy Cramer.*

This Austrian warship fired the first salvos at Belgrade on July 29, 1914. *Public Domain.*

down in their shallow dug trenches on Mt. Cer. Soon the gun boats would aim in their direction. They nervously watched the Sergeant give the order to fire. But he shook his head. "Too far. Hold on for a closer shot. Every bullet must hit its mark," and he pointed to his old Ottoman style musket.

Townspeople fled the streets and wharves, hiding in the cellars and basements in houses farther away from the rivers. Some militia poured out of stores and cafes, carrying their Ottoman muskets and bandoliers. They sought safe places where they could begin loading and firing, continuously loading and firing.

From across the river, The Soldier looked on in amazement. The gun boats were turning around, while others were battered to pieces. Austrian gunners who had fallen into the water were desperately trying to reach the far shore before the sharp eyes of the Serbs sighted them and aimed their guns at them.

The fear that had almost paralyzed the Serbs on the mountain vanished as they saw the scene of their invaders' defeat. They rose as a group and cheered their brothers across the water. A victory, but so soon? That could not be possible, a victory against the great monarchy of Austria-Hungary. Was it a trick, an ambush?

The Sergeant followed their thoughts and blew his whistle to round up his men and make their way back around the mountain peak to their headquarters. "What do you think happened?" Misha asked Pietro, who shook his head. "I don't trust those Austrians to give up so easily. Anyway, maybe it is true, and I can go home to my wife and children now. I don't like this fighting. I'm gone."

"But that's deserting. You can't leave, especially now that we've won our first battle." Pietro picked up his musket and kit and strode off in another direction, careful that the Sergeant didn't see him. The Soldier watched the men assemble to hear their commander. But he saw others slip off to the side as Pietro had done, The Soldier shook his head.

VICTORY AT MT. CER

The Serbs won their first decisive victory in the battles for Mt. Cer and surrounding villages during August 15-24, 1914. They were victorious despite having 70,000 fewer soldiers than Austria-Hungary. Its soldiers were improperly garbed, lacking the simple upturned toe boot or *opanki*, regular uniforms, and caps called *sajkacas*. However, many Serbs were experienced fighters and highly motivated. Those who were unarmed fought with pitchforks and axes until they could find abandoned rifles and ammunition.

Voyoda Radomir Putnik commanded the army along with Generals Stepanovic and Sturm. The battle began at 11 p.m. August 15 when Serbs from the Sumadija Division came upon some Austrian outposts on the slopes of the mountain. Fighting in the darkness turned into chaos, and in the morning the Austrians retreated in disorder. The following morning the Austrians attacked but failed miserably and the Serbs inflicted great damage to the Austrian ranks. The Sumadija Division continued to hold its own.

Another village fell as the Serbian First Morava Division and the Third Army shattered the lines of both the Austrians and Hungarians. The Serbs were accustomed to fighting in the mountains and used that terrain to their advantage. The battle ended when the Serbs, having surrounded the heavily fortified town of Sabac, found that the enemy had decamped during the night. The Serbs had driven the Austrians to the Sava River and ended the first invasion of the war.

However, the cost was high with 3,000 Serbs killed and 15,000 wounded. For the enemy, the loss was much higher with 8,000 killed and 30,000 wounded and a loss of 46 cannons, 30 machine guns, and 140 ammunition wagons. All these were desperately needed by the Serbs. Reports of Austrian atrocities were collected by Serbian General Sturm, leading to the reprisals of months and future years. A group of 19 Serbians including women and children were roped together and "horribly massacred. Another mass of 15 people were found in similar condition, as well as small groups of slaughtered and disfigured people. Belts of skin and even breasts of women had been cut off. This was commonly found among villagers."(Source: Andrej Mitrovic, 2007)

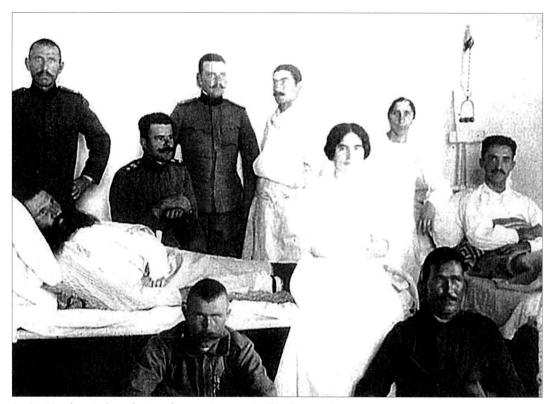

An Austrian hospital ward, site unknown. *Courtesy Bosiljka Stevanovic.*

AFTER THE BATTLE OF MT. CER
A Story as Envisioned by the Author

"Look, look they're retreating! I can't believe it!" Radomir turned excitedly to his friend, Bozidar, and pointed to the left of where he was half standing, half squatting in a trench. Other men gathered around, peering in the half darkness of early evening. At the base of the mountain below them, they could see the Austrian-Hungarian soldiers marching at a fast pace in the opposite direction.

"What do you think that means?" Bozidar asked. "Is the war over?" he asked with hope in his voice.

"I don't think so, but at least we won't be fighting them here for a while," Radomir said. "Here comes the Sergeant, maybe he knows something." The men rushed over to the weary Sergeant who was coming toward them with long strides.

"Tell us what is going on," they asked, almost in one voice. The Sergeant answered patiently, "It means that we have driven the enemy off Mt. Cer, with the help of our friends, the Montenegrin soldiers. We formed an alliance with them and some new fighting units—the Sandzak Army and the Drina Attachment. They liberated Pljevlja on

the first day, then other places. Also our army liberated Sabac. The headquarters says that's the first victory for the Allied forces since the War began a month ago. And we Serbs did it! You men can be proud of yourselves." He was interrupted by the men cheering.

"Hey, I'm not finished. Now for the bad news. We've got hundreds of dead Serbs lying on this mountain. Tomorrow we will form teams to find and bury them. Then, you'll get some kind of leave. But no slacking on the burial duty. I know it'll be unpleasant for some of you since you've got friends and maybe relatives out there, but they deserve a decent burial, and my platoon and some others are assigned to do it. I want it done with dignity and pride. We Serbs are soldiers to our last breath, and those lying out there have taken that last breath. Now, for supper and then into your blankets. You've got a hard day or two ahead."

The men had stopped cheering while the Sergeant spoke. What he said was true. There were too many friends and neighbors from the village out there in the darkness that had fallen. Too many families back home would be grieving soon when the word gets to them. How could each man take pleasure in a leave at home now. Now, with so many dead ones to remember.

Four days in August the Serbs battled the Austrian-Hungarian army at this site. The 180,000 Serbs were greatly outnumbered against the Austrian-Hungarian armies of 250,000, but they won the desperate battle, shocking the outside world. The Austrian-Hungarian armies retaliated in nearby villages with numerous crimes against the civilians, killing at least 4,000. The total casualties from the battle also were great. This monument was erected in 1928 in the village of Tekeris. The four "C" shaped letters on the front below the crown, with two of them backwards, stand for the old Serbian Empire and its components. *Courtesy the Panacorp Wonderland Travel Serbian Agency, Serbia.*

"When the going got tough, the tough started singing." This is how these Serbian troops could march long distances for long hours. *Public Domain****.

FIRST VICTORY FOR ALLIES IN WAR

The use of Austrian airplanes for the first time to observe Serbian positions was almost futile. This was because the Serbs concealed gun positions and men under the trees of the vast forests. In addition, the mountain sides deterred the ability of the Austrian flyers to fly safely.

The First Morava Division and the Third Army recaptured villages and in doing so, shattered the unity of both the Austrian and the Hungarian soldiers.

THE WINNER
A Story as Envisioned by the Author

The Soldier watched the men as they entered the old stone hut. Each one dropped his kit and rifle, scattering them on the bare floor. Wearily, they stretched out, using the kit as a pillow. Djornik wanted to shed his great coat. The itching of the lice had worsened. His hands shook as his fingers fumbled with the large buttons. He had to get his coat off. The harder he tried, the more his hands trembled. The lice had itched him all day. Now was his chance to get rid of them.

He nervously tried the next button. No success. Then the next button. He reached the hem of the long coat, all the buttons refusing to give way. With a shout, he jumped up and ran out the makeshift door, rolled in the snow, sobbing. The lice had won. His skin was on fire. He tore at the top button again, pulling it off the fabric. Then he pulled at the next button until it gave way. He was sobbing and ripping the coat like a mad man until his older friend, Utrick, came out and stopped him.

"Old fellow, settle down. You'll ruin your coat. Let me help you." Utrick's calloused fingers gently opened each button until Djornik could pull his arms out of the coat. "The lice. The lice are burning my skin," Djornik sobbed as he scratched wildly. "I've got to get rid of the lice." The commotion caused the other men to gather. They stared helplessly at their friend. They, too, suffered from lice, but they just endured them.

What had happened to Djornik on the trek up the mountain? Was it the sight of his three friends blasted into hundreds of pieces, and seeing their flesh and clothing scattered everywhere on the snow? Djornik had wanted to gather up the larger fragments, the bones with flesh clinging to them, the ribbons and buttons from the uniforms. But there was no time to wait. That shell had located the end of the squad's line, and soon other shells might find the rest of the squad. They changed the direction of their climb. It was useless. The Austrians had good field glasses, and the Serbs' dark uniforms were easy to spot against the white snow. Somehow, they managed to escape the increasingly close fire of the Austrian artillery.

Each one of them had seen bodies shattered by shells. Everyone had endured the long hours of continuous bombardment from the heavy Austrian field guns. Yet Djornik was the only soldier acting like a crazy man.

The Soldier observed the whole scene. "Too much, too much for Djornik," he thought. "Djornik has reached his limit. Now the Sergeant will have to reprimand him and send him back to headquarters in disgrace. No Serb wants to be called a coward or crazy." He turned and left the hut. Utrick was still trying to calm his friend before the Sergeant arrived.

MUSIC OF WAR AND DEATH
A Story as Envisioned by the Author

Old man on his one-stringed gusle instrument played songs of both joy and sadness. *Drawing by Vivian Kallmann.*

The soft mournful music of the instrument drew The Soldier from his thoughts as he walked through the darkness toward the sound. He soon saw a campfire with soldiers lying or sitting around its warmth. The player was old, from the Third Ban, and of the age to be the grandfather of any of The Soldiers. He played the one stringed instrument with such feeling as to draw various emotions from his listeners. The minor key brought forth the sadness of the song he was singing about a Serbian hero.

The instrument, a gusle, was familiar to The Soldier, having heard it in his youth when he shepherded sheep in the mountains near Bitola, his birthplace. The Austrians were now approaching Bitola, and the sound of their guns signaling a night attack were an ominous comparison to the quick, lively tones of the gusle and the singer's voice rising to tell of the victory. Surely the soldiers and the player were aware that soon they would be fighting the enemy or fleeing into the safety of the hills. Maybe this music would calm their anxiety and remind them of the victorious fighters of the past. Perhaps it would remind them also of the homes and families left behind to fend for themselves as best they could.

The Soldier relished the last long drawn out tone on the one string of the gusle. He saw the player carefully wrap it in its animal skin cover. The other soldiers slowly got up, picked up their kits and their rifles. They too knew not only was the music over, but that they were going to hear a different music soon—the ominous sounds of war and death.

DISASTEROUS BATTLE OF THE RIVER DRINA

Enraged by Serbia's refusal to agree to all of the ten terms of Austria's ultimatum issued July 23, 1914, the Austrian-Hungarian Government declared war against Serbia on July 29, 1914. This signaled the beginning of a war that would spread throughout Europe and to the other faraway continents. It also meant for the Serbs, the start of a series of campaigns that by 1916 would result in the occupation of their country by the invading forces of the Central Powers. This story describes the events that led to the Battle of the River Drina in September and October 1914. This Battle began a reversal of Serbian fortunes continuing until October 1918 when the Serbs and their Allies defeated the Bulgarian army which surrendered.

Even before the declaration of war, the Austrian government had conducted an unusually brutal campaign against the Serbian minorities in Bosnia and Herzegovina. These people had been annexed to the Austria-Hungary empire a few years earlier. On July 26, 1914, hundreds of former Serbs in these two neighboring states were arrested. Martial law was imposed in neighboring Slovenia. Fifty ethnic Serbian citizens of Dubrovnik, a city in Albania, were executed, and in Austria, some Serbian-Czechs were beaten. One consequence of Austria's cruel behavior resulted in thousands of the Austrian-Hungarian Empire's two million ethnic Serbs crossing the borders and enlisting in the Serbian army. However, if the ethnic Serbs were captured fighting later for Serbia by the Austrians, their fate was usually immediate execution.

The Serbs' victory at Mt. Cer was followed by the Austrians marching through the summer heat, and then retreating when falsely told that the Serbian army was just behind them. Chaos ensued, and every man thought only of preserving his life. The dead and wounded were left behind. As one writer observed, "They trampled over each other in their haste." By the evening of August 24, the only Austrians left in Serbia were the 4,500 prisoners under Serbian control.

This humiliation of the Austrians by the Serbs led to recriminations and harsh measures by Austrian military leaders against their own soldiers. In their customary punitive fashion, Austrian officers took extreme disciplinary actions. Those who had immediately eaten their emergency rations, causing great hunger later, were tied to trees and exposed all day to the summer sun. In the meantime, small skirmishes against the remaining Austrians in Bosnia were made by forty battalions of Serbs and their ally, the Montenegrins.

A Serbian field-gun and team in action, firing from a concealed position inside a culvert. *Public domain, courtesy Dr. Matt Osborne.*

In the interim, before the next invasion by the Austrians, the Serbs examined their strengths. They were used to fighting in the mountains. The local partisans or *komitadji* would come to their aid. The Serbian army did not recognize "social classes" as did the English. Serbians would repeat: "We are all peasants in Serbia, this is our pride," meaning that even high ranking officers had no special social position above the lowest private. Relations between the ranks were more of a comradeship than a strict separation.

Some problems were serious, such as the lack of rifles. Only two-thirds of the mobilized men had arms. Special groups were appointed to search homes and confiscate rifles found there. Some privately owned guns had beautiful carved silver ornamentation, which probably caused Grandpa some anguish, although perhaps with pride that he could help his country by handing over his treasured gun.

Another problem was lack of uniforms. About 200,000 were needed. The soldiers were instructed to wear their civilian clothes until the uniforms could be procured. However, the traditional three-cornered style Serbian hat, *sajkace*, was available for all to proudly wear. In a stroke of luck, the Serbians had obtained some modern 15 cm howitzers, far superior to the old 10 cm guns of the Austrians. The Serbians also badly needed four wireless transmitters to facilitate communication.

Despite formidable problems, an important strength for the Serbs lay with the commander, Voyoda Radomir Putnik, an elderly but formidable and experienced leader. He was crafty and had a good knowledge of the landscapes and the best strategies to use. However, he was severely ill with asthma, and his poor health required that during the Retreat he had to be carried in a sedan chair by soldiers who frequently rotated in groups.

Destroyed artillery from the disastrous Serbian loss at the Drina River. The Serbs again were outnumbered in men and especially artillery. The steep rocky hillsides made inadequate trenches for the oncoming Austrian-Hungarian shells, of which they had an ample supply. *Photo courtesy the Panacomp Wonderland Travel Serbia Agency, Serbia.*

Serbs Retreat to the Mountains

A second invasion was begun by the Austrians on September 2, 1914. By now the incompetent Austrian General Potiorek had a Slovak guide for each regiment. But he had no control over the changing weather and the nature of Serbian rivers. They can be mild in spring and summer, but in the fall and winter, they become wild and raging. Storms called *Kossava* made crossing them hazardous, if not impossible. The Serbs, however, did not shy from such battle conditions. As the ancient national poem proclaims: "I am a Serbian, born to be a soldier."

Several disasters occurred for the Austrians, including the incident when the Serbs bombed a newly built bridge, crowded with celebrating Austrian musicians. All died in the explosion. The Austrians later retaliated in a surprise attack against the Serbians, pushing them back to establish another bridgehead. Voyoda Putnik recalled the First Army from Syrmia, against the advice of his generals. However, the First Army delivered a bloody drive against the Austrians. The drive finally stalled. An extremely costly four-day battle in late September followed. This was to secure the peak of a mountain named "Mackov Kamen." Both sides experienced terrific losses. The Serbians and Austrians each suffered about 11,000 casualties, but the Austrian force was depleted temporarily.

The Serbs took advantage of the Austrian weakness and retreated to the mountains where they spent a miserable six weeks in the shallow trenches. Their footwear, the traditional *opanki*s, were made of soft pigskin which was not suitable for the rocky terrain or trenches. Loss of life was high, about 100 men per day, resulting from shelling by the Austrian guns, which were well aimed at the trenches. The Serbs were unable to find the protection they had anticipated by moving to the mountains. On a brief excursion into nearby Bosnia, the Serbs, supplemented by the Montenegrin Sanjak Army, a division in strength, dug under the Austrian trenches. These trenches were only about 20 to 30 meters (about 65-90 feet) from the Serbian trenches. The Serbs and Montenegrins planted mines and set them off just before their infantry charged. This was the first time the Serbians had used land mines in the war, and the results were devastating for the Austrians.

Total losses at the Drina River were 18,500 Serbs and 17,000 Austrian-Hungarians. Though the Serbs were defeated here, they nevertheless regrouped for the next battle, which was to be at the Kolubara River. Here the story had a different ending.

THE BATTLE AT KOLUBARA—SUCCESS AT LAST!

After two major campaigns at Mt. Cer, the Serbians drove the Austrians back. This fighting and the battle at the River Drina exhausted both armies. However, the shrewd strategist Voyoda Putnik saw an opportunity to widen the pincer noose the Austrians were tightening around the Serbian armies in the western lands. Putnik staged another retreat. This one had the army fighting as they marched, hoping the Austrians would move deeper into central Serbia. His strategy worked.

The road system, already primitive at its best, was now a quagmire due to autumnal rains. Austrian supply lines were disrupted, and movement of its larger guns almost came to a standstill, although the smaller ones could still be moved. Personal reports kept by Austrian troops described the lack of food, rest, and supplies. One such writer, Josef Sramek, a Czech soldier, told of packages of food from home being stolen by the sergeants, and the officers getting drunk and beating the men with sticks. The men even lacked water. Josef concluded his complaints with this remark, "Being in the army is getting tougher day by day."

Serbian soldiers marching from victory at the Kolobura River. *Public Domain. Courtesy Dr. Matt Osborne.*

King Releases Men from Their Oath

The Austrian General Potiorek misread the Serbian army's difficulties as being part of its last attempts at resistance. He captured the town of Valjevo on November 15. The Serbs abandoned Belgrade, and moved their government to the city of Nis (Nish) on November 29. Putnik, after a conference with King Petar and other generals, decided to use the mountainous terrain as a last stand against the enemy. His troops were skilled at using mountains as a defense, as they had demonstrated at Mt. Cer. King Petar, meanwhile, in an humble but sincere speech, offered his troops the opportunity to leave the army without disgrace or prosecution. He released them from their vow to serve him. As for him, however, his choice was to stay with the army until its last days.

In Vienna, the capital of the Austria-Hungary empire, the citizens were rejoicing and celebrating, thinking the war would be over in a matter of a few days. Their army would return home victorious. What they did not know were the miserable, almost starvation-like conditions their troops had to endure, such as only half a loaf of bread for each man every three days. Dysentery was affecting large numbers of troops, and the changing weather conditions were bringing snow and rain.

Potiorek's efforts to continue to extend his army were prohibited by Voyoda Putnik's expert control of his armies' movements. In addition, ammunition from France had arrived in the Greek port of Salonika and was brought to the front by rail. Timing was crucial. The arrival of artillery shells allowed Putnik to make a surprise counterattack. He did this on December 2 and gained a few miles from the overstretched Hapsburg forces, which had failed to establish strong defensive systems. This, combined with poor morale and physical health, and other factors, weakened the resolve of the Austrians. Another Serbian offensive the next day caused the Austrian line to collapse.

By December 14, 1914, Belgrade was back in Serbia's hands, as were thousands of Austrian prisoners, as many as 60,000, some historians say. To the disappointment of fellow Slavic soldiers in Austria's army, they were roughly treated by their Serbian kinsmen. By now, the Serbs had heard of the Austrians' brutality meted out to innocent civilians, the old, the young and women. The Serbians were in no mood for forgiveness. Too many of their own kinsmen had been tortured, beaten, shot, hung, and otherwise badly treated. Now was the time for retribution and revenge.

The rest of the world saw the proud Austrian army march home in defeat. The small nation of Serbia had shattered the Hapsburg's arrogant reputation as being one of Europe's finest armies. However, now the Serbs had to face another enemy, one that was insidious and almost invisible. That was the disease called "spotted typhus."

THE SERBIAN AIR FORCE

It was a surprise to the world when the tiny nation of Serbia introduced their first aircraft in 1912. It was unbelievable that this "backward" nation would become the fifth nation in the world to form an air force. The Serbian military in 1909 purchased two balloons, and the first six pilots went to France for training. Once again, Serbia's leaders were anticipating what were the best ways to defend their country. Aircraft, including balloons, was still in the background of military might. The first bombs to be dropped

The first armed airplane of the Serbian Army in 1915. The airplane is a Bieriot X1-2,the pilot is Tomic, and the observer is Mihajlovich. *Public Domain.*

were by the French on an oasis in Libya in 1911 where Turks were stationed. Little damage was done but the idea of attacking from the air had become a reality.

The first Serb pilot to complete his training, Mihajlo Petrovic, unfortunately, became the second pilot to be killed in the World Military Aviation group, as it was named. He died on a combat flight. His pilot's license was number 1. The first pilot to be killed was the Bulgarian Topradzijev, who died on his return from a reconnaissance mission over Edirne, Turkey. It was during the invasion of the Serbia by Austria in October 1915 that the future famed pilot, Manfred Von Richthofen made his first flight as a pilot. He was known as "The Red Baron," and became the pilot with the highest number of "kills" during WWI.

During the war with Austria in 1914-1915, Serbian pilots served valuable roles in observation and reconnaissance, especially in the battles of Mt. Cer, Kolubara and the Drina River. In 1915 the pilots added machine guns and small hand dropped bombs to their planes, as did the Allies and Central Powers on the Western Front. The Serbian pilots were instrumental in attacking the enemy planes that flew over Serbia, in addition to bombing Austrian targets. A Serbian artilleryman became the first soldier to shoot down an enemy plane when the Germans made an air attack against the city of Kragujevac on September 30, 1915. The artilleryman aimed through the bore on his gun and brought down the German Farman plane with its two crew members.

The French Air Corps joined the Serbians in April 1915 to try to gain control of the skies but the German offensive led by General Mackensen began in October 1915. Meanwhile, Serbian craftsmen were producing planes in furniture factories, using French made motors. These were named "PINGVIN" or "Penguin class," and only a few planes were made.

Another first for Serbian aircraft occurred when the army began its historic Retreat in the fall of 1915. French and Serbian planes were used to carry wounded soldiers back to hospitals. During the Retreat, the planes helped maintain the important connection with the retreating troops along the Albanian coast to Durres and Vlore. The services these pilots offered demonstrated the value of airplanes to the military. Their usefulness was shown again in 1916 on the Thessaloniki front line in Greece. More modern aircraft and weapons had become available to the Serbian and French pilots, thus increasing their effectiveness and skill in the air. Unfortunately, the Austrians retaliated by shooting and bombing the survivors of the Retreat as they waited exhausted on the Adriatic beaches for ships to rescue them.

It was in the fighting on the Salonika front that the Serbian Air Forces were re-born, assisted by French pilots. A Nieuport division was formed by the end of 1916, and in 1918 the First and Second Serbian Fighter Escadrilles performed many flights assisting the ground forces.

Once again, the Serbians made up for the small size of their country with large ideas that worked.

WILL HELP COME FROM THE ALLIES ?

Letters expressing the Serbs' desperation were sent almost daily to the French and English, reminding them of the great disparity between the sizes of the armies of the Austrian-Hungarians and the Serbs. The most crucial need was ammunition and guns for the Serbs. At first, the answers were all positive. A letter from King George V of England, with his royal signature and seal promising that aid, is prominently displayed in a Belgrade museum.

Meantime, the Allies had their own problems that they determined outweighed the needs of the tiny Serbian army. Large numbers of the huge French army of 1,250,000 men and 200,000 British and Belgian troops faced 85 German divisions comprised of almost as many men. The Allies needed to make a breach on the Western Front to stop the Germans from advancing to Paris.

To add to the Serbs' dilemma, the Russians were pleading for assistance against the Turks. It was then, after dozens of ideas were examined and rejected, that Winston Churchill's proposed invasion of Gallipoli was seriously considered. The Serbs were out of luck, despite the accolades of being "a fierce warrior people steeled by an intensive national patriotism." (Palmer).

It took only two weeks for the Serbs to liberate Belgrade and drive the Austrians out of Serbia. This "Miracle of the Kolubara" brought Serbia once again to the attention of the Allies. But to shorten the story, despite the ferocity of the Serbs and their tremendous loss of men, 170,000 killed and wounded and perhaps 50,000 ill with typhus, the Allies delayed for months before assisting the tiny nation. That action consisted of the futile attempt by the French to invade from the south. Here, they were deterred by the mountainous terrain and lack of transportation. In terms of troops and armaments, they arrived too late with too little men and supplies.

Despite some unexpected victories in the north at Mount Cer and elsewhere, Voyoda Putnik made the only decision he believed that would save the Serbian nation. That decision was to retreat by three main routes, adding a fourth one later, to Albania. There on the shores of the Adriatic Sea, Allied ships would rescue survivors and transport them to the Greek island of Corfu. These would include troops, civilians, boys, and medical teams who survived the long trek of as much as 400 miles for some Serbs.

They would be taken to the Greek islands of Corfu and Vido to recuperate. Serbia's King Petar accompanied the army, often riding on horseback or driving an ox cart. The stalwart 70-year-old monarch buried the royal signatories of the Serbian nation on the Serbian side of a mountain separating Albania and Serbia.

Historical Precedent Set

Voyoda Putnik, the army commander, was ill with asthma and other afflictions, but he also was determined to accompany his troops on the Retreat. He was carried by loyal soldiers in an enclosed chair to keep him protected from the harsh winter air. The carrier teams rotated every 45 minutes to rest from the effort of slugging through snow and ice, up hills and mountains. The valiant Voyoda Putnik survived the rigors of the journey to Corfu but was sent to France where he died in a year or so later. Greece finally was persuaded to fight the Bulgarians in the land between Greece and Bulgaria and bordering Serbia. However, later Greece reneged on its agreement.

Voyoda Putnik probably was not aware of the historical precedent behind his decision. The decision not to surrender. Instead, to escape and re-form an army to fight the enemy again. This decision was to be only the third time in recorded history that a country had taken this strategy, despite hundreds of wars during the past 2000 years. Zenophon, the Greek general, was the first to use this military strategy in 400 B.C. fighting the Persians. The second time was in 1800 when Napoleon retreated from the Austrians, then was reinforced by an attachment of French troops who had been recalled from their earlier dismissal. With the additional troops, Napoleon fought the Austrians and was victorious at Marengo.

If Voyoda Putnik had been informed of this history, what would his reaction have been? Possibly, he would have shrugged and said something like: "How stupid of the generals not to have thought of this strategy. It is so simple what we have to do."

Voyoda (Marshal) Radimir Putkin, head of all Serbian armies. He was in ill health and with asthma and other lung problems, but accompanied his troops the entire Retreat. He was carried in an enclosed sedan-like chair by four men show rotated positions regularly because of the difficult muddy and snowy roads and the climb across the mountains. He died in 1917 in France where he had been hospitalized *Public Domain****.

PART FOUR

THE TYPHUS EPIDEMIC

THE WORST TYPHUS EPIDEMIC THE WORLD EVER KNEW

The typhus epidemic began in mid-December 1914 and spread rapidly. It peaked by March 1915 and then began subsiding, partially due to the humanitarian aid offered by medical personnel from many countries. The British were especially notable on the scene. Officials from other nations had come to inspect the results, noting that dead bodies were piled up on straw in buildings outside the villages. Hospitals had tents full of men with post-typhus gangrene. This is a condition in which the flesh rots away, leaving only the bones which then crumble. Estimates of Serbians infected reached as high as 400,000. Some 30,000 soldiers died, as did about the same number of Austrian prisoners of war held in Serbia.

The Serbian government imposed a number of restrictions to help prevent the spread of the disease. Schools were closed; public meetings cancelled; and except for small units of soldiers, leaves for most the military were cancelled. Troop movement was held to a minimum. Civilians were forbidden to travel, except for medical personnel. The war raging on the Western and Eastern fronts resulted in all types of supply shipping routes to Serbia. The governments of Greece and Roumania blocked caravans of necessary medical supplies until under strong persuasion by the Allies they relented for humanitarian reasons to allow passage of the caravans. Roumania and Russia later became victims themselves of the epidemic that spread when their soldiers went into combat with the Austrians.

Aid from Around the World

Lady Leila Paget, wife of Lord Ralph Paget, chief of all British units of assistance in Serbia, opened a large hospital in Skopje, Macedonia. **Countess Trubetskoy**, wife of the new Russian minister to Serbia, brought in two field hospitals and badly needed supplies. Two bacteriologists were sent by the Rockefeller Foundation and the American Red Cross. The French, always the friend of Serbia, sent 100 physicians from its own dwindling supply. Other aid came from Sweden, Switzerland, Italy, Denmark, and the Netherlands. From distant countries such as Japan, Argentina, and Chile, volunteers came to bring the total of more than 2,000 other nationals aiding Serbia.

There were no medicines to treat the disease. Medical personnel used cold vinegar compresses and aspirin to alleviate the high fevers of the victims. [Today preventative medication can be taken if one is traveling abroad to an area prone to typhus. Medications can treat and usually cure the disease.]

The humanitarian desire to help was not without its risks. Almost 500 aid workers died of typhus, and other workers contracted diseases that were fatal. Meanwhile, reports to Germany of the number of Serbian deaths were received as welcomed news. However, the international world, in a show of solidarity, joined together to fight this ruinous epidemic. The cooperation of the Allies and their supporters was essential as the Great War entered the destructiveness that characterized 1915, the second year of the war.

WHICH WILL IT BE? TYPHUS OR THE BULGARIANS?
A Story as Envisioned by the Author

Miles away, men from the Sumadija Division labored on their way home to their villages. Like other army units, the group became smaller as they walked on. Sometimes, those too weak to continue were taken by peasants who had a place for them in their overcrowded ox carts. Other times, a medical unit ambulance car laid the men on the floor of the car and took them to their tent hospital for treatment. Again and again, the same sights appeared of burned houses, fields with large craters from artillery shelling, and groves of fruit trees devoid of limbs.

In one horrifying scene, the Sumadija Division men saw the bodies of peasants hanging from crosses, still unburied and smelling of decay. Ox carts, filled with dead bodies, their legs dangling from the sides of the carts, passed by the soldiers. One village was completely empty of its inhabitants, save one elderly man whose mind was deranged. He finally was able to tell the incredible story that all the residents of the village had died of the typhus, although due to his mental condition, not everyone believed his story. A few curious soldiers peered into many of the houses. Some were filled with decaying bodies, and the stench was overwhelming.

"It's true, true what he says," Vladan said excitedly. "They are dead, just lying there and stinking up the whole place. Let's get out of here! I don't want to catch the typhus, let's go!" he said, picking up his kit and rifle and started down the road alone.

"Wait, wait for me," another soldier called. "Let's get away from this work of the devil." The rest of the group followed. One man shared part of his loaf of bread with the old man, and poured water into a leather bag sitting beside the beggar. Each man was relieved as his village came into sight. Some buildings were badly damaged; other villages on paths located away from the main road, appeared almost untouched. Evidently the Bulgarians, in their haste, destroyed just those on their main route.

As a soldier neared his village, his breath shortened. Others felt his tension. Would there be any of his family left to greet him? Would his house still be standing? The men had been together through many terrifying and death invoking experiences. They were like brothers. One could not rejoice openly when he found family and home safe, knowing that other men would be sorrowed, even crazed by what they found on arrival. They were bound by the bond of war. They all shared the other's potential fate.

HE DIED OF TYPHUS AS A BULGARIAN PRISONER
Interview With Boban Zarkovich by Mail

Boban Zarkovich's grandfather died of typhus while a Bulgarian prisoner in World War I. Boban, a Serb who now lives in California, tells this story of his grandfather and also of having met a *Solunlac*. There had been a disastrous typhus epidemic in Serbia in 1915 and about half a million civilians and soldiers died, mainly in Serbia, but also in Roumania and Russia. Requests from the Serbian government for international help were generously answered by many nations.

England sent the Scottish Women's Hospital group and other medical teams. France helped with the International Red Cross, while Americans sent money and American Red Cross medical teams. This was the world's worst typhus epidemic up to that time. It was believed to have started during 1914 when an Austrian prisoner, sick with typhus, was interned. The extremely contagious disease is spread by bacteria-carrying lice. It can be eliminated in one site, but as long as people traveled or were transferred, and were infested with the lice, they spread the disease. This happens when the tiny lice attach themselves to the clothing, especially in seams or the lining. They attack the human body and inject the harmful bacteria through biting.

For years, doctors had no evidence as to what caused the disease. Finally, a doctor isolated the bacteria and was able to prove that lice were the culprit. The first step was to thoroughly clean the hospital rooms and homes where sick people lived. Then wash their clothes in boiling soapy water and scrub their bodies with hot water and strong soap to rid them of the lice. Thanks to the hard work of cleaning and scrubbing every house and habitat, boiling clothes daily, and use of disinfectants, the medical teams and Red Cross volunteers were able to bring the epidemic under control.

Fortunately there was no fighting going on at that time. The Serbs had defeated the Austrian attacks in 1914. The Austrian soldiers quickly retreated back to Austria and their homes before the lice started spreading. Typhus usually resulted in a painful, ghastly death, especially if the victim was in poor health to begin with.

Typhus Victims Lost Will to Live

One hundred years ago there was nothing more than aspirin and vinegar compresses to treat typhus. In one small Serbian village a chapel was built to honor the dead children. In the novel *Reach to Eternity* by Dobrica Cosic, the Serbian author writes that after one bite from a louse, (scientific name *Typhus exanthematicus*) people often gave up. They lost their will to live. The international medical teams, by eradicating the lice, helped restore the Serbian morale. The soldiers' motivation to defend their country was high now that they were well. When the Austrians attacked again in 1915, the Serbs, despite being greatly outnumbered and outgunned, won some big battles. Finally in the end of that year, they chose to retreat to save their country rather than surrender.

They went to Corfu island where they recuperated and were trained by the French to use modern weapons. Then they were transferred to Salonika, Greece, from where they fought the Bulgarians along the Serbian/Bulgaria borders.

Bohan, the Serbian descendant, also writes about once having met a *Solunlac*. This was the name given a Balkan soldier who fought on the *Solunski* front from 1916-1918 (the Salonika front). The *Solunlac* soldier that Bohan met was then in his 90's and unable to tell Boban much about his experiences in the terrible battles against the Bulgarians. Much of the fighting took place in mountainous areas where the Bulgarians had installed machine gun nests and heavy artillery. The Serbs and other Allied soldiers had to climb ladders sometimes to gain the high mountain reaches where the guns were hidden.

The mountain rocks and small trees cleverly concealed the machine gun nests. It took the grim determination of the Serbs to clear out gun emplacements from the various levels of rocks and overhangs. By now the Serbs were filled with revenge, not only for their own suffering on the march to freedom in 1915, but for the many stories told of Bulgarian atrocities against the Serbian families and their priests. This war only multiplied the hostile feelings of both nations.

THE NEWLY MADE WIDOW
A Story as Envisioned by the Author

"Knock! Knock!" came sharp, rapid sounds on the cottage door. Jovana put down her mending and went to the door, lifted the latch, and peered into the twilight. Young Tomas, the son of her neighbor, stood there. He looked weary and his uniform was muddy and torn.

Jovana said, "Come in, come in. Can I fix you some coffee? I thought you were at the front at Morava with all the other men from the Morava Division. What news do you have?" she excitedly asked. Young Tomas said, "You better sit down, and if I may, I'd like to sit down too. I've walked 22 kilometers from the battle site, and I have some news you may not like." Seeing her face grow worried in the light of the kerosene lamp, he thought, "Why do I have to be the one with such bad news? Why couldn't the Sergeant come?" But he knew the Sergeant had been shot in the leg and was needed at the front, despite his hobbling around with the painful wound.

Jovana put the kettle on the iron stove, thinking, "Bad news, it can't be for me—not about my husband and sons. They are strong and promised they would return when the Austrians and Bulgarians are defeated. It must be about one of the neighbors." She turned and tried to smile, her heart beating anxiously.

Young Tomas eagerly lifted the cup of coffee she handed him. It smelled tempting, although it wasn't real coffee. No one, especially the army, had real coffee, but the smell of the ersatz was strong. "How should I begin?" he thought. "How will she take the news?" He sipped the coffee slowly, trying to make the time pass before he had to reveal his tragic message.

Finally, he blurted out, "We fired at the Bulgarians, and they saw the flash from our gun. The Bulgarians then fired a flare and aimed at our battery. Just then the moon came out from behind the clouds, adding to the light. They zeroed in on our battery, hitting all of us in the pit. The pits were shallow because we couldn't dig deep in the rocky ground, and they gave us no protection. The shelling hit all of us, that is, except me. I was holding the officers' horses back behind the trees. Everyone in the gun pit was blasted to bits. There weren't enough pieces to bury even a single body."

He was interrupted by her shrieking. It seemed to come from deep inside her body. "All of them—you mean my man, my sons, everyone? Some must have escaped."

"No," he shook his head sadly. "We were very close to the Bulgarians when we positioned our guns. After we fired, we moved back quickly, but the Bulgarians had the light from the flare and the full moon to help with their aiming. They fired a direct hit. Even the men in the back who were bringing up new shells were killed by the artillery blast and the shattered rock. It was terrible, terrible," and he began sobbing.

Helpless to stop, she screamed again, "Mother of God, have mercy, have mercy."

Young Tomas was startled by her outburst. He spoke rapidly without even thinking about his words. "I'll go get the village priest. Some of the women will come. You can live at our house while my father and I cross the Albanian mountains with the other Serbian soldiers. There the Allies will rescue us," his voice trembled. "Then later we will come back and defeat the Bulgarians." He paused.

"My mother, you remember her, died of the typhus last year while Father and I were away in the army. We've been without a woman in the house ever since. Oh, please, stop crying. Stop crying. I'll go for help."

Jovana didn't hear Young Tomas. She sat in old willow chair, rocking back and forth. She covered her eyes with her hands, and moaned. "Oh, Mother of God, have mercy, have mercy. How could this have happened? Have mercy."

Young Tomas took one last sip of the cold coffee and silently slipped out of the door, pulling the latch behind him. The newly made widow continued crying and rocking, while Tomas desperately sought some neighbors to come help.

The Soldier stood in the darkness, unable to comfort Young Tomas or the widow.

KRALJEVO—THE TOWN THAT SURRENDERED

Kraljevo was a town of great military importance for both the Serbs and the Germans. It was important for the Germans because the town had the largest munition plants in all of Serbia. The capture would deprive the Serbs of the badly needed ammunition they lacked. For the Serbs, its surrender meant they had to depend mostly upon the dwindling supply of shells shipped by the British and French. The Serbs, after the town's surrender, retreated southward the Fall of 1915. Before they left, however, they had blown upon the bridge that led to the city. Unfortunately, it was only partially destroyed, and the enemy quickly repaired it enough to allow their troops into the city. The Serbs had loaded their ox carts with as much ammunition as they could carry before they retreated, but it was only a fraction of what they would need in the next few months.

Harsh Surrender Terms

Once the Germans entered the city, they proceeded to the railroad station, meeting stiff resistance from the Drina II Division of Serbs. Finally, when the Germans seized the crucial railroad hub, the city officials had to submit to terms of surrender. The booty captured by the Germans included 130 guns which had been loaded onto railroad cars which stood on the tracks. The Bulgarians earlier had severed the main rail lines, stopping all Serbian rail traffic. Other supplies included valuable automobiles, wagons, searchlights, aircraft, fuel, medical equipment, and the priceless stock of food.

The truce meeting with the German commander must have been agonizing and humiliating for the Mayor Stojkovic. Part of the surrender terms included payment of $110,000, a large sum of money for the population of 7,000 citizens to raise. This money was to be compensation to the Germans for "reparations for the damages the Serbian soldiers had committed." Adding the money to the valuable military supplies, the Mayor Stojkovic was forced to agree to the substantial surrender terms. The townspeople were desperate.

The town leaders had made a difficult moral decision, but a decision that must have saved countless lives and many properties from damage. It was the elected leaders' duty to protect their citizens from needless harm, if at all possible. Although the Serbs were desperate for the ammunition they destroyed, they knew the Germans would have used it against them immediately, or perhaps against the townspeople of Kraljevo as the enemy had done previously in numerous other villages in their path.

Under the terms of surrender, the Germans accepted the money and did not plunder, rape or destroy the city. The town leaders had made a difficult moral decision, but protecting its citizens from known intended harm was their first duty. However, for the Mayor, to hand over the key to his city to the enemy was certainly the most difficult act any mayor had to perform.

LOSS OF NIS AND KRAGUJEVAC

To Voyoda Putnik, only a few options remained. The weather, the notorious muddy roads, and quickly advancing enemy troops were drawing the noose tighter around the Serbian soldiers in the center part of Serbia. The Voyoda had made desperate decisions before. This would be one of the most difficult in his career. The Germans had joined the Bulgarians in approaching Nis and Kragujevac, despite the many bridges the Serbs had dismantled, the swampy roads, and rivers overflowing the banks. Serbian troops were being taken prisoner by the hundreds as the enemy overcame them. Serbian resistance and morale were at one of their lowest points.

One choice had been to make a stand at the border of Macedonia, but that plan had failed. A second decision would be to abandon both Nis and Kragujevac because the Voyoda did not have enough troops in place to defend both towns. The third option had been quelled when the Serbian government refused to sign a separate peace from the rest of the Allies, so only one solution remained. That was to leave Serbia.

The soldiers in the field discussed among themselves which option they preferred. No one wanted to be taken prisoner. "To be captured by a Bulgarian meant perhaps torture first, and certainly a death sentence," Sergeant Nemanja explained. Germans might not kill the soldiers but would send them to concentration camps or deport to Germany to work in labor gangs.

TO BE CAPTURED OR TO RETREAT TO ALBANIA?
A Story as Envisioned by the Author

The soldiers in the field discussed among themselves which option they would prefer. No one wanted to be taken prisoner. Sergeant Nemanja explained, "To be captured by a Bulgarian meant probably torture first, then certainly a death sentence." He added that Germans might not kill the soldiers but would certainly send them to concentration camps in Germany or to work in labor gangs there.

Milos asked about getting help from the Allies. But as the Sergeant emphasized, "The trains, what are left of them, are under enemy control. We can't move any equipment ourselves because the good tracks are in the enemy's hands. The bad tracks, well, they are very bad tracks. Just rails scattered like pins. So be prepared to carry on your back what you need." A groan arose from the men.

When the official word of the capture of the two cities was announced, Serbian morale was at its lowest point. Even the officers had difficulty hiding their feelings from their men. When marching through their own towns and villages, the Serbs took the hay and portable goods and food they needed, but they would not leave the peasants completely destitute. The Germans, however, had no such paternalistic feelings. Because of where the Germans were fighting in Serbia, they were not allowed to receive packages of food and clothing from their homes. As a result, they seized what they needed or wanted from the conquered.

Putnik's army, by forced march, despite the continuous rain and its effect upon the roads, managed to escape the noose by which German General Falkenberg had intended to trap the Serbian army. Instead, the army took the Retreat route toward the towering and treacherous Albanian mountains. The Germans, rejoicing in the capture of Nis and Kragujevac, believed new paths of communication and movement were now opened for the Central Powers. They were misled into thinking the noose had tightened. Once again, the wily and clever Serbian leaders and soldiers had outsmarted them.

The Soldier, watching the Serbians take the dangerous route to the west, had a grim smile of pride for his men.

Wounded Serbian soldiers, who were unable to walk, rode in ox carts or early ambulances, which often became stuck in the mud. Oxen were unhitched to pull the ambulance or auto out of the mud. *Public Domain.*

PART FIVE

ENGLISH MEDICAL
HELP ARRIVES

FIRST STOP—MALTA

A Story as Envisioned by the Author

Malta. The name brought up pictures of green trees and grass and the steadiness of land under her feet. Dr. Elsie Inglis clung to the rail as the ship rose on another swell. Malta, not Serbia, was to be their next destination. Their task now was to set up a hospital for the wounded from Gallipoli, instead of wounded Serbians. Her mission had been to serve the Serbs, and she was impatient about the delay in reaching them. As the supervising matron, she wondered if her girls would be up to nursing the wounded at Malta. Few of her forty British nurses had seen men freshly wounded from combat. The nurses had usually served in hospitals behind the lines where wounds had already been cleaned and bandaged or covered with casts or splints.

The Scottish Women's Hospital Team was one of the first and most important medical teams to come aid Serbia in 1914 when the typhus epidemic was rampant. They returned the next year to care for war wounded Serbian soldiers, even following them on the Retreat. *Photo of Scottish Women's Hospital Team – Public Domain.*

Now her nurses would see blown off body parts, profuse bleeding, and heads split open by shell concussions. Perhaps even some patients with brains spilling out. But nurses were urgently needed in Malta to care for the tremendous flood of the wounded Allied casualties from Gallipoli. She shook her head.

Of course her nurses could face it. They were British, mostly Scots, with one or two Irish mixed in. They had the best training she could offer, and they were young and strong. Their good humor and anticipation of the new assignment had kept most of them from being homesick. The few that regarded the seriousness of their assignment had kept their anxiety to themselves.

Men in Royal British Navy uniforms scurried around the decks, preparing the ship for landing. Dr. Inglis went into the main room where the nurses had assembled. Her girls were lined up, baggage at their side, blue cloaks fastened at the neck, and white caps with veils covering the back of their hair. They were talking and laughing. A few, still suffering from motion sickness, sat quietly on benches. "Yes," Dr. Inglis decided, "They can do it. They have to. We are the only nurses these wounded soldiers will have."

When Would They Get to Serbia?
A Story by the Author Based on History

The sailors rowed small boats toward docks and helped the nurses with bags and baggage to climb down the steps into the boats, then rowed them to the beach. Horses hitched to wagons stood by, and soon the nurses filled them all. The horses headed off at a trot, as if they too, were in a hurry for the nurses to see the hospital.

Soon, wooden buildings, newly constructed, appeared, and the horses stopped to unload their passengers. The nurses looked around at the bare grounds, wondering what the buildings looked like inside. From the outside the buildings had no resemblance to a hospital. They were more like barracks or a dormitory. Dr. Inglis went to the head of the line where the Minister of Health was waiting for her with a high ranking army officer. They introduced themselves, and the minister said, "Dr. Inglis, I am sure your nurses want to get settled and have a rest before tea. This building will be their dormitory. The other buildings are the hospital."

Their long journey to Serbia from England was, of course, delayed now. But how long would they be here, they asked each other? When would they get to Serbia? What if the fighting destroyed the one railroad in Serbia that ran north and south, the one that would take them to the battle zones? Questions flew from the eager young women.

"Patience, my dears, it will all happen in good time," Sister Enid, one of the experienced nurses answered. "Now it's on with our tour." One by one the forty nurses followed Dr. Inglis and the officials to see what was to be their new home. For these nurses, the final trip to Serbia would have to wait.

Previously, once Dr. Inglis and Dr. Hutchison had established the hospital in France at the Abbaye du Royaumont, they hurried to Serbia in late 1914. There they confronted the raging typhus epidemic that affected military and civilians alike. There was no known treatment or medications for typhus at the time, however, the Scottish Women's Hospital was practical in their handling of patients, their homes and the hospitals. In wards with 200-300 patients, it was impossible to stop the spread of this highly contagious disease.

MILLIE AND THE YOUNG SERBIAN SOLDIER
A Story as Envisioned by the Author

Sister Bridget called from the next room. "Millie, I need your help. We are overwhelmed with the wounded, and I need assistance." Millie straightened her head covering, pleased that Sister Bridget asked for help and that she could leave washing the bloodied bandages for a while. Wiping her hands on a special towel for that purpose, she was reminded how particular the Scottish Hospital Women were about every detail. Nervous, Millie hurried to the room where a young Serbian soldier lay on a cot. He was about 17 years old, scarcely older than she was. His torn uniform was covered with blood, and his face was scarcely identifiable because of all the wounds.

Millie took a deep breath and moved to the side of the soldier, who was moaning and semi-conscious. She glanced at his uniform which was full of holes as if a mountain wolf had clawed the soldier. Then, she stopped, aghast at what she saw. Little pieces of metal stuck out all over his body, including his bare hands and face. The metal pierced the cloth like giant sewing pins. He moved slightly, then gave a loud groan.

Millie heard a voice, coming as from far away, telling her, "Don't stand there, Millie dear, wash your hands in the disinfectant. Then hold the pan while I pull the shrapnel out of his body. Now hurry, he is in great pain, and we can't make him comfortable until the metal is removed."

Millie turned to the basin of disinfectant, dipped her hands in the water and rubbed them. Nausea was rising in her throat. The room seemed to spin around her. She had never seen a body so badly wounded. How could she possibly help Sister?

"Come, come, it's a bad sight I know, but you are up to it, Millie girl, and I have no one else to help. Now hold the pan steady while I pull out the pieces," Sister said. With long surgical tongs Sister, slowly, one by one, gently removed the shrapnel and dropped it into the tin pan. It clinked each time. Clink. Pause. Clink. Pause. The soldier opened his eyes once, then closed them with a long sigh.

Millie wondered as she held the tin pan full of sharp pieces, "Is he dying? He can't be. He is too young. He has a life to live, and so do I after this terrible war is over. Don't die, please don't die." Sister continued the long tedious process, sometimes stopping to staunch the blood that flowed from a wound opened by the removal of the shrapnel. Frequently she reached for the pile of clean bandages and applied them, until it seemed his chest and arms were covered with white patches.

Finally, Sister stopped. The shrapnel was all removed. She poured iodine onto a clean bandage and gently wiped each wound through the holes in his uniform. The soldier winced with the sting of the iodine, occasionally opening his eyes but seeing nothing. His moaning was low and continuous.

"Now Millie," Sister Bridget instructed, "take the pan to the dumping box and empty it. Be very careful, the shrapnel is sharp like your father's stropped razor. Then come back and help me finish binding the wounds." Millie obediently went to the rear of the building where there was a wooden box to hold the pieces of shrapnel and bullets taken from many bodies. She dumped the pan, then rushing to a nearby bush, she leaned over and vomited, again and again. She heard Sister calling her. Millie wiped her mouth on her apron, straightened her back, and went to the room where the young soldier lay, waiting to be bandaged.

She knew then she could do it. And she would do it over and over again, with each newly wounded soldier.

BRITISH WOMEN BRING MEDICAL CARE TO SERBIA

Mrs. Mabel Stobart, Dr. Elsie Inglis, and Lady Leila Paget

These stamps were issued in 2015 to honor six English women who served valiantly during the fighting and subsequent Retreat. *Courtesy the Serbian Postal System.*

Once the war between Serbia and Austria officially began, England and France immediately asked what help Serbia needed in health care, weapons, and ammunition. The United States also investigated, and quietly assisted, but remained officially neutral until April 1917. Posters and rallies were held by the hundreds in all three countries to raise money. The medical professionals determined what aid was required and began organizing it. Anticipating the treatment of war wounds, they learned that by the winter of 1914, a more insidious problem existed. It was an epidemic of typhus, the most serious the world had ever known.

Along with the military doctors, there were two women's organizations and a third woman by herself who would later achieve worldly respect for their accomplishments in Serbia. One was the Stobart Hospital team, led by the stalwart **Mrs. Mabel Annie Stobart**, an administrator but not a physician. The second group, the Scottish Women's Hospital, was headed by **Dr. Elsie Inglis**, an administrator and also a surgeon. Her group of women filled all positions except those of orderlies, for which men were recruited. The third English woman was an aristocrat, the **Lady Leila Paget**, wife of the former British representative to Serbia, who worked in similar healing capacities.

Mrs. Stobart wrote about her work in Serbia in a book, *The Flaming Sword in Serbia and Elsewhere.* She begins her story in 1914 when she was asked to return to the Balkans. She had previously provided nursing services in Bulgaria for the First Balkan War of 1912. She was later appalled by the reputed Bulgarian atrocities during that war and excused herself from serving there further.

Instead, she answered the call of the Belgian Red Cross to go to Brussels, already occupied by the Germans. The continued aggression of the Germans made it impossible to establish an Allied hospital there. Mrs. Stobart and her companions were arrested and sentenced to be shot within 24 hours. Somehow, they managed an almost impossible escape, after being lectured by the German in charge. He shouted, "You are English, and, whether you are right or wrong, **this is a war of annihilation**." (Stobart) Those disturbing words remained with her for days. After escaping and returning to England, Mrs. Stobart learned that the St. John Ambulance Association and parts of her own units had not yet departed for Serbia.

Mrs. St. Clare Stobart, left, confers with an associate about her plans to establish a war hospital in Serbia in 1915. *Public Domain.*

Beauty of Serbian Countryside
A Story as Envisioned by the Author

Soon Mrs. Stobart's groups were on their way to set up a hospital in Cherbourg, France, on the coast of the English Channel. Meanwhile, in Serbia, the typhus epidemic began to get out of control. One-third of the Serbian doctors had perished from serving at the front or from typhus. The need for more nursing and medical help in Serbia was critical. Mrs. Stobart went to London to work her way through the red tape and bureaucracies with which she was becoming familiar. She requested and was granted funds and by February 1915, she and her units immediately began the long, difficult and dangerous journey to Serbia. They sailed from Liverpool, England, to the Greek city of Salonika, on the coast of the Mediterranean Sea. From they rode on the only north-south railroad in Serbia to the strategically important city of Kragujevatz, where she administered the first Serbian-English field hospital.

Her team included seven women doctors, whose presence would astonish the peasants who came for help. "A woman doctor?" they asked incredulously. Serbia was mostly a rural country, consisting of small villages and farms. The people had little access to education, with illiteracy possibly as high as 80%. Tradition and superstition replaced knowledge of hygiene and good health habits. This meant the English medical teams had to teach their Serbian patients about modern medical practices and the importance of cleanliness, as well as treat their illnesses.

As they traveled on the old train, Mrs. Stobart described in her book, *Flaming Sword...* "the local countryside with glowing appreciation of its beauty." Little did she know that months later it was to be a place of death for hundred, even thousands, of fleeing Serbs. She described the "picturesque one-storied houses of sun-dried brick, mountains, rivers, gorges—with clean air, warm sunshine and blossoming fruit trees." But occasionally the scars of destroyed villages and newly dug graves marred her admiration of the countryside. Each river, each gorge with its ancient Ottoman style steep arched bridge would in the near future provide an obstacle to the refugees. Because the bridges were coated with ice and snow in an unusually early onset of winter weather, the refugees sometimes passed over with difficulty, injury or falling to their death.

Peasants in Dire Need of Medical care

Eventually, Mrs. Stobart set up six hospitals within a radius of 30 miles of Kragujevatz. All the hospitals consisted of tents, both for convenience in erecting them and for sanitary reasons. Sometimes, however, the frequent rain and storms brought water leaking through holes or gaps in the tent. This left the occupants with wet bedding and garments. Still, the tents served the purpose of easy erecting and dismantling, a feature that proved important when the artillery guns worked their way too close to the hospitals.

In vivid words, she described the serious medical conditions of the peasants who flocked to the compounds. Diphtheria was one of the worst, with some people dying in the wagons that brought them, too late for help. Other peasants, too old or too ill to travel in the make-shift wagons or even wheelbarrows, were to die in their far off mountain cabins. Several times fathers would bring sick children, and when asked why they had waited until the condition was almost fatal, their sad reply was, "I just arrived home from the front yesterday." At first, a few peasants scorned using the hospital, saying "Why, she is much too ill to go to a hospital!" They would take the child away, hoping for the best, and the poor young one probably died on the way home in the slowly moving cart. This attitude quickly vanished as other peasants who used the hospital recovered from severe illnesses or wounds.

The children loved being patients in the hospital, and under the kindness of the nurses, the good care and food they ate, most of them flourished. Many became upset when told they were well and could go home now. As well as dealing with the desperate needs of the sick civilians, the unit continued its primary mission to treat the wounded soldiers. The team simply added more tents and doubled their work load.

In November 1915, the Serbian army no longer had the strength and manpower to protect the city with its ammunition plants. The oncoming Austrians initiated the beginning of the massive Serbian retreat to Albania, hundreds of miles from this centrally located site. The march took ten weeks under the most difficult of conditions. Nevertheless, Mrs. Stobart, astride her famous black horse, led her faithful group of peasants and wounded soldiers to the edge of the mountains. Many wagons had lacked covers during the onslaughts of freezing rain, thick snow storms, and roads that were constantly muddy. There she had to give up her horse and walk the treacherous paths of the mountains. She could take only a few medical supplies to be used. The people, soldiers, and medical teams retreated over the mountains, sometimes walking continuously up to 25 hours to keep ahead of the enemy.

At Pristina Mrs. Stobart was assigned a group of 80 people. They walked for 81 consecutive hours with only short rest periods until they reached Dresnik, where they camped at a deserted farm. On December 3 they began the ascent of the mountains, using only ponies to carry what few items could be loaded. "Men by the hundreds lay dead: dead from cold and hunger by the roadside…no one could stop to bury them…it is believed that not less than 10,000 human beings lie sepulchered in those mountains." (*The Flaming Sword.*) They reached their final destination, San Giovanni, on December 19, after crossing Lake Scutari in a motor boat and riding in bullock wagon to San Giovanni. From there they took a steamer to Brindisi and a train through Italy to Paris, arriving in London on December 23.

It has been estimated that more than 100,000 people died during the Retreat, but Mrs. Stobart's group would claim that all her followers made it safely without any deaths or desertions. Some soldiers and peasants decided, unwisely, to take a chance on returning to their nearby farms, hoping for favorable treatment by the enemy. Many of them regretted their decision as attested to by the atrocities committed.

These atrocities were noted and brought to the attention of the world after the war ended, but as sometimes happens, justice was ignored and the perpetrators were either dead by then, or many were not persecuted or punished. However, the Serbs had a long memory, and vengeance occurred in the mountains of Greece and during the Salonika campaign which began in 1916 and ended with the Bulgarians' surrender in October 1918.

Before the war even ended, the skills and kindness of these doctors became legendary, as did those physicians from the Scottish Women's Hospital. Both groups and their medical teams personified the reputation of the English for courage and fortitude in the face of great difficulties. That reputation lives on today in grateful Serbia, as well as for all the other English medical personnel who saved Serbia in her "time of troubles."

SCOTTISH WOMEN'S HOSPITAL UNITS LED BY DR. INGLIS

A Story as Envisioned by the Author

Dr. Elise Inglis

"Now, let me count. Nurses—38 of them; bullock carts and oxen; automobiles; dispensary kits…" and so Dr. Elsie Inglis inventoried her medical team and supplies as they approached Valjevo on the final lap of their 45-day journey by sea and by land from England to Serbia. Austrian prisoners unloaded their boxes and crates and carried them as directed by one nurse to the makeshift grounds of the hospital that soon would consist of the various tents set on the hilly grounds.

Dr. Inglis laughed to herself as she recalled the remarks of the pompous English official who had addressed her as

"My good lady" and told her to go home and sit still when she offered her medical services to the English army. Sitting still was one thing Dr. Inglis had a problem with. Pompous officials were another, but she soon learned how to handle them and overcame the red tape that often delayed her plans.

Dr. Inglis's organization had international recognition. For years she had been successful in establishing hospitals for women in the British Isles. The French military, desperate for medical help from the start of the war, asked Dr. Inglis to set up a hospital in the immense historic Abbaye du Royaumont near the Oise River in northern France where most of the fighting was taking place then. Dr. Inglis enlisted her friend, **Dr. Alice Hutchison**, to head the unit of the Scottish Women's Hospital at Royaumont. It was to be complete with operating rooms, a dispensary, and even x-ray rooms. It was enormous, with 600 beds and an auxiliary casualty clearing station at nearby Villiers-Cotteret. Then Dr. Inglis returned to England to raise 30,000 pounds (English money) to start a new hospital in Serbia.

That enterprise and additional ones would add to her role as an historical figure in providing medical services in World War I. She established 13 hospitals in total throughout war zones in France, Belgium, Serbia, Greece, Macedonia, Russia, and Roumania before she returned to England, where she died shortly after her arrival.

A strict disciplinarian, she set high standards of cleanliness in the hospitals. These standards the previous year had helped curtail the typhus epidemic. She was held in highest esteem not only by her medical staff, but by medical professionals in England and France as well. Her staff and medical professionals in France and England respected her because of these medical practices.

Only disinfectants were available, thus limiting the curtailment of germs and infections. Next, the lice, attached to the clothing were killed by boiling the garments in hot soapy water. However, the eggs buried in the clothing seams were destroyed by special sprays. The men were sprayed also. This epidemic began in late 1914 and within four or five months, it was brought under control in Serbia, moving on to Roumania and Russia. Dr. Inglis returned to England to learn where her next assignment would be.

Dr. Inglis was a suffragette also and believed that women should have an equal place in society. Her role as one of the first female surgeons to be allowed in military hospitals illustrates her determination. She also influenced young women. Records show an appeal from a Miss **Elsie Bowerman** on July 5, 1916, in which the young lady asked her mother for permission to go as a driver with Dr. Inglis.

A small publication, *Predstrazha Serbaki,* or *The Serbian Outpost*, written by **Dr. Alice Hutchison** from Serbia where she was a physician, tells stories of the Scottish Women's Hospital and its experiences during 1915-1916 at Valjevo. She led the third hospital unit which landed May 28, 1915 at Salonika, Greece. Her hospital would be the "third blocking hospital in northern Serbia." These hospitals would be near the major battle scenes. The morning after the medical team landed, the group took the only train that went into Serbia from Salonika. Traveling throughout Serbia was primitive because there were so few railroads.

Here Comes the "Roughing"
A Story as Envisioned by the Author

Dr. Hutchinson described the stops at train stations which were crowded with dirty, ragged Serb soldiers, battle weary but still displaying the good manners for which they were noted. Aboard the train, they rode past "shell-shattered buildings, hill-sides scarred with trenches, and…group(s) of rough crosses marking the graves of the fallen." They arrived in Nis in late evening, and learned to their disappointment that "high waters had made the bridges impassable that they were to cross. That meant another night in the shabby town." However, a group of Austrian prisoners presented a musical program for the guests "that might well put many professional British performers to shame." Dr. Hutchison went to bed thinking that now they were facing the first of the "roughing" that they had been cautioned about.

Because most of the volunteers had signed up for only a six-month service, ending September 30, a meeting was convened in Kraguevatz to discuss the staffing situation due to the unknown outcome of the war. The decision was to leave all existing units in Serbia, with no more English units arriving. The recent entry of Bulgarian troops into Serbia was helping to close the gap in a pincer type movement that could easily entrap the Serbians in the southern part of the country. The medical teams would be in great physical danger if that occurred. Meanwhile, most of the Serbian troops were away from the Valjevo area, but there was much need among civilians for medical care. Dr. Hutchinson's journal noted "foreign missions have perhaps years of heavy work before them, if disease and want are to be banished from this beautiful devastated land." Little could she imagine the great trial they would soon embark on to leave Serbia.

Several of the doctors and nurses became seriously ill with an enteric illness. The cooks, meanwhile, heard the disturbing news that the supply of sugar was to be rationed to one-half pound per person per week. The English were fond of very sweet tea, and this was a blow to their morale. "No sugar for the tea?" was a common complaint.

By July 5, 1915, the Hospital Unit No. 2 had completed setting up its hospital in Valjevo and received its first patients with more arriving. There were to be at least three SWH in all. The invalids were transported in slow oxcarts marked with a red cross. Wounded soldiers came limping in a long procession, painfully dragging their bodies. They were dusty, dirty, clad in bloody tattered uniforms, often with either worn out boots or no boots at all. As quickly as possible, they were washed with the soap the soldiers had lacked and provided with clean uniforms or hospital garments.

Communicating in the different languages proved a difficulty, but often "dobra" (or good) meant almost anything. The nearby French mission, which served the town's civilians, needed another nurse and was sent one of the SWH nurses. More SWH nurses filled in as needed in the other French and Serbian hospitals located there. Ultimately there were hospitals at both Mladanovatz and Lazaravatz. Five years later the Serbs erected a fountain at Mladanovatz in memory of Dr. Inglis and her Scottish Women's Hospital personnel.

Packing Up and Always Retreating

The Allies continued their efforts to reach the Serbian armies but obstacles were too great to overcome. The British forces had been stopped from a western advance into Serbia, but the French succeeded in making a charge up the Vardar River Valley with its strategic railroad. However, the Bulgarians, who had entered the war on October 20, 1915, diverted their assaults on Serbs in the south, and instead, ended the French advance on November 20 on the Vardar River Valley. By December 12, all Allied forces gave up their efforts and returned to Greece. The last hope for outside Allied help for the Serbs was extinguished. The Serbians were on their own.

The first SWH team never knew how long they would stay when they set up their tent hospital. When the enemy approached the rear Serbian guard too closely, word was sent for the medical team to pack up and move with the Retreat. Other humanitarian groups in Serbia suffered the same fate. The hospitals established in Uskub by **Lady Paget** had fled. However, the **English Ambulance Corps** and Lady Paget stayed and were taken prisoner by the Bulgarians, along with some nurses who had refused to leave the wounded on their own.

All the medical teams at Valjevo began the final packing up of oxcarts and loading of wagons. The staff of the other two hospitals in Ladanovatz and Lazaravatz also packed up quickly and joined Dr. Inglis at Kraguyevatz. From there they divided into two groups, with one group becoming part of the Retreat. Others of the team stayed in Kraguyevatz with Dr. Inglis to care for the Serbians too severely wounded to be moved. They endured nights of incessant shelling, but because Dr. Inglis remained calm, the panicky feelings of others diminished. They lived on constant rumors of Germans attacking or the British coming to the rescue.

Despite the "wretched condition of the men," the women reveled in the "beauty of the sunrises (and) the glory of the sunsets." It was at Czar Lazar Hospital in Kraguyevatz that Dr. Inglis and Dr. Hollway and others were captured by the Germans in November 1915 and taken prisoner. All the women slept in one room and listened to rumors of impending bombing raids. Dr. Inglis calmly ignored them and fell asleep.

The hospital was vacated February 9, 1916, with "chronic" invalids sent to their homes. Most of the seriously ill men had been taken to hospitals in Hungary. The remaining few severely wounded who would be invalids for months were taken to the Austrian hospitals for further treatment.

On February 11, under Austrian guard with fixed bayonets, the rest of the Scottish Women's Hospital teams were sent north. They were under strict orders not to communicate with anyone while traveling. However, they met a Serbian woman in their waiting room in Belgrade who had no fear of the Austrian officer in charge. He said if they spoke in German, they could talk to her. She wanted news of her husband, which the women happened to know. They reassured her that he was getting better.

"Vrylo dobra (Very well)" she said over and over. They repeated what she had said, and the officer laughed. He obviously lacked an understanding of the Serbian language.

The group finally reached Vienna, where they were released to the American embassy. They proceeded to Zurich, Switzerland, "our hearts sick for the people we had left behind, still waiting and trusting."

Dr. Inglis continued her work once she returned to England, speaking about the tragedy of the Serbian people, raising funds for services to them, and working to send a unit to Mesopotamia, scene of the British fighting against the Ottomans. In August

1916, she left for Roumania, where she again engaged in similar work as in Serbia. The hospital there had been established to help the Jugo-Slavs in the Austrian area, fighting the Russians who took them prisoner. The Russians freed them at the request of the exiled Serbian government to form Serbian fighting units against the Germans. These were men of Serbian heritage but lived in lands formerly conquered by the Austrians and had to join that army. Once they were in Serbian uniform and under Serbian command, they fought valiantly against the Bulgarians, although with great loss of life. One unit of 14,000 men, at the battle of Dobrudja in Roumania, had only 4,000 Jugo-Slavs who survived.

Doctor Elsie Inglis Dies in England

Dr. Inglis continued to work under difficult conditions and retreated three times from the Germans. Where the SWH stopped for the last retreat, in Braila, Roumania, there were 11,000 wounded and seven doctors. Only one was a surgeon. Her skills became invaluable again.

She faced many obstacles while trying to get her unit out of Russia in 1917, now that the Russian Revolution had begun. At last, on November 23, 1917, Dr. Inglis and her unit arrived in Newcastle, England. She had been very sick during the whole sailing. "She had been dying for months," a report stated. She died soon after she returned. Dr. Inglis was buried with full military honors in Edinburgh, her former home. The service ended with the "Hallelujah Chorus," the "Last Post," and Royal Scots buglers "rang out the Reveille." A friend was heard to say, "What a triumphal home coming she had!"

Indeed, triumphal and incredible. She had managed to persuade the Russians to release all the Serbian soldiers who had been fighting in Russia and allow them to come to safety in England. However, many continued to fight and die in battles with the Germans and were never to see their homeland again.

Dr. Elizabeth Ross

Another distinguished English woman physician, **Dr. Elizabeth Ross**, became a victim of the disease she had gone to Serbia to help its victims. Dr. Ross had been working in Persia since 1909, when she learned of the great typhus epidemic that had stricken thousands of Serbians. She immediately volunteered her services at Kraguyevatz, where she was assigned to the First Military Reserve Hospital. The conditions there were "shocking," according to her remarks. Unfortunately on her 37th birthday, February 14, 1915, she died of the disease. Her grave in Kraguyevatz is located next to two other British medical aides who also died of typhus. In 1980 the townspeople restored her grave and held annual commemorations every February 14 to honor her and all the other foreign women who died assisting the Serbian people. It has been estimated that at least 600 foreign volunteers came to Serbia to bring aid, and that 22 of them perished in their work.

Meanwhile, in Serbia, government officials, who had set up temporary headquarters in Nis, fled westward toward Mitrovitza. They had no means of communicating with the various Serbian forces or of knowing where the enemy soldiers were at any one time. All the officials knew was that they had the responsibility of sending the men who made up the Serbian government, including King Petar and Prince Aleksander, to the safety of Albania.

Other medical teams followed the Serbian troops who had fought near their location, although some teams left the severely wounded in hospital tents with volunteer medics to tend to them. These personnel were captured, but through the efforts of the International Red Cross, most were repatriated within three to six months. During their internment as prisoners of war, reports say that most were not ill-treated.

Other Reports About the Retreat from Medical Personnel

A British war correspondent, **Gordon Gordon-Smith**, was in Lipljan when reports were made of advancing Bulgarian soldiers. He was traveling with a companion and met three French Red Cross nurses, accompanied by a Russian military doctor and his staff, all who were headed toward Prizren. Gordon-Smith and friend teamed up with a section of the Scottish Women's Hospital, also headed for Prizren in their ambulance. Before they could start their journey, Gordon-Smith, using his field glasses, saw some Bulgarian shrapnel bursting along the top of the hills. Bulgarian troops had penetrated the Serbian lines and were firing on the railroad station about 300 yards away from where the SWH had parked their ambulance.

A Serbian cavalry unit was camped near there. When they heard the firing, they rode to the station, dismounted, and began shooting the Bulgarians. However, previously during the night, the Bulgarian firing had alarmed the Scottish women, and they decided to leave in their ambulance in the darkness. The hapless Gordon-Smith and his companion had to walk the distance to Prizren.

Most of the medical personnel retreated by walking. A few were able to ride in ambulances, but often there were delays caused by flat tires, broken parts, or being stuck in the glue-like mud. The feet of oxen and people had churned the wet dirt roads into deep troughs. Some automobiles slid off the mountain paths down into crevasses, resulting in death or injury of the passengers. Finding shelter for the night, especially after the *knosse* (snow) began again, was often left to chance. **Miss Tatham, an English Sister** as nurses in England were called, (See story p. 81) wrote that twenty of them slept at Rashka in "an awful little hovel … in an indescribably filthy room, over a stable full of Army horses, and next to a larger room in which they were making shells!"

Another night was spent in a hospitable Albanian hut, crowded with refugees, soldiers, and nurses. The livestock of the farm also shared the same quarters to be safe from the freezing temperatures outside. Miss Tatham wrote, "My neighbor on one side was a warm and comfortable calf!"

A British nurse, **Sister Olive Aldridge**, commented, when passing the first corpses by the roadside: "Five men were stretched out stiff and lifeless across our path. Nobody took any notice of them; all passed by, just stepping over or round the dead bodies…" Her driver of the ox wagon said, "Niye dobro (not good)." Many Austrian prisoners on the road begged for bread. She had none to give the pathetic starving men.

She commented, "It was terrible…we knew that within the next few days they would be dead…never to see their homes or their country again."

By the time the civilians reached the mountains, many of them changed their minds at the sight of the fearsome mountains and started to return to their homes. Hundreds, perhaps thousands, of soldiers also changed course and deserted. The king had released them from their oath of service, so "deserted" does not appropriately describe their actions. The women remaining in the Retreat were mostly nurses and provided what medical aid they could with the few supplies they had packed on mules. Mules had been purchased at great prices because the mules' feet could grip the ice and snow better than the horses' hooves. Most of the horses had been left behind, and many were near starvation. In addition, the mules could survive on less food. There was little food to be found in the solitary areas of wintry mountains for man or animal.

For the peasants and other civilians, the Retreat meant robbery, even murder, at the hands of the roving Albanian thieves. Some Albanians in their anger even took axes to chop off heads and limbs. These men still wanted revenge from the war of 1913 and proceeded to practice some of the worst criminal acts against the helpless, weakened Serbs. Many families, as a result, turned back to try to reach their homes, only to suffer even more brutalities at the hands of the Bulgarians. The actions of the Bulgarians were so heinous that after the war, investigations were made and punishment, when possible, was meted out. Regrettably, the feelings of hatred and fear between the two countries could not be extinguished easily and existed for many years after the war ended.

OTHER ENGLISH WOMEN WHO HELPED

Lady Leila Paget - English Humanitarian and Nurse

The third woman notable for her devotion to the Serbians and one who almost lost her life there was **Lady Leila Paget**. She had lived in Serbia earlier when her husband was the British representative there. Her first contact with the British military medical staff had been in 1912-1913 during the Balkan Wars, when she helped to establish a military hospital in Belgrade. She returned to England after the wars. But it was when she learned of the Austrian invasion of Serbia, that she decided against the advice of her husband and friends to give up her safe, luxurious life in England. She chose to endure the hardships of becoming a volunteer nurse.

Lady Leila Paget

She arrived in Serbia in November 1914 and traveled to Skopje, where she offered her services to the large British medical mission there. The typhus disease had made its appearance there, bringing in hundreds of soldiers for treatment. Lady Paget herself later became one of the infected patients. Fortunately for her and for the Serbians, she recovered after spending time recuperating in Switzerland. By July 1915 she was well enough to return to her beloved second homeland, Skopje. The Retreat began that fall, and after the hospital had evacuated all but the most serious cases, she made the courageous decision to stay behind with those patients.

Bulgaria by then had occupied Skopje, and finally, after all the wounded were sent to other hospitals, she returned to England. She left behind a letter which expressed her deepest feelings: "I have always had warm sympathies toward Serbia and Serbian people, and there was always some kind of a specific bond between them and me, that made me think of them with love, even when I'm far away from them, a bond that made me come to Serbia with the same amount of joy as when I went back to my home. Once again and truly, thank you all, and see you again."(Serbia. com/ Serbian Literature)

Unfortunately, because of the events of the oncoming years, she never saw her beloved Serbia again.

Dr. Isabel Hutton
Served with the Scottish Women's Hospital

Dr. Isabel Hutton

Dr. Hutton, otherwise known as Lady Emslie Hutton, was another woman doctor rejected by the Royal Army Medical Corps. But like Dr. Inglis, she sought out the Scottish Women's Hospital and offered her unusual training as a psychiatrist. At first, she was needed as assistant medical officer and pathologist in 1915 and worked at a tent hospital in Troyes, France. Soon, she and her team were sent to Serbia, then on to Salonika, Greece, arriving in December 1915.

Her services required transferring to other hospitals, until finally, in October 1918, she moved to Vranja, Serbia, after the Bulgarians signed a peace treaty. She remained in Vranja for a year, setting up local hospitals, then moving to Belgrade and working until 1920. She helped Lady Paget's Child Welfare Scheme in the Crimea. Her last official military hospital position was in Sebastopol, but because of the Russian Civil War, the hospital evacuated to Constantinople. There she championed the cause of aiding Russian refugees. Like the other women discussed in this book, she received a medal, the Serbian Order of the White Eagle, for her many contributions.

She returned to England in 1920, but during World War II, she traveled to India where her husband was stationed. Her last work involved directing the Indian Red Cross Welfare Service and other organizations.

She recorded in her notes while in Serbia and Greece, "As soon as a Serbian person recovers, he starts to sing and dance. This was in his character and an integral part of life; just as tilling the land. Their favorite song was "There, Far Away.".…Some of us women sang together with the soldiers…and got to like that beautiful language." She, like so many of the English medical people, loved and admired the Serbians, and Serbia became her second home. (See p. 90 for this song)

Dr. Katherine S. Macphail
Orthopedic Surgeon in Serbia

Katherine and her sister, Isabel, followed their father's profession of medicine in an era when few women were allowed to practice medicine. When the Serbian-Austrian war began in 1914, both sisters joined the Scottish Women's Hospital team. Women were not allowed in the armed forces of any country, but this team (see story about Dr. Elsie Inglis p. 37) provided valuable medical service for Serbia. After helping to establish the famous French hospital at Abbaye de Rayaumont, they moved on to Serbia. Isabel was assigned to be an orderly and Katherine, a surgeon.

Dr. Katherine S. Macphail

Neither women was a suffragette as many were in the SWH, but they found a common bond in offering medical relief to Serbia. However, when Katherine arrived at the main SWH in Kragvejvatz, she was disappointed not to be offered a position for which she was uniquely qualified. She transferred to the Belgrade Military Hospital, which incurred the displeasure of the SWH. Nevertheless, she spent her life working in Serbia.

After the war she established her own small hospital, the Anglo-Serbian Children's Hospital in Belgrade. For her war service she was awarded the Serbian Order of St. Sava and the Serbian Red Cross. In 1928 she was honored by the English with the Order of the British Empire. However, she felt there was still work to be done, so she set up in 1934 a hospital for Osteoarticular Tuberculosis in Sremska Kamenica. Her work continued there until 1941, when she and other British residents were captured by the Germans. She was released and returned to England, but in 1945 after World War II ended, she again returned to Belgrade. During this time foreigners were not as welcomed, and she left Serbia for the last time in 1949. She died in 1974, a "heroine in war and peace." (University of Glasgow-Story and Biography)

Evelina Haverfield
English Suffragette Becomes Serbian War Worker

Evelina Haverfield

There is a headstone engraved in English in a small remote mountain Serbian town. This is the way the spelling and punctuation reads:

"Hear lies the body of the honourable Evelina Haverfield youngest daughter of William Scarlette 3rd Baron Abinger and Helen ne Magruder his wife of Inverloky Castle Fort William Scotland who finished her work in Bajina Bashta March 2, 1920 through the war 1914-1920 She worked for the Serbian people with untiring zeal. A straight fighter a straight rider and a most loyal friend. R.I.P."

Evelina was a member of a suffragette group, which at the war's beginning, founded a Women's Emergency Corps and also a Women's Reserve Ambulance Corps. After helping for a short time, Evelina left and joined the Scottish Women's Hospital as a hospital administrator. When the group, headed by Dr. Elsie Inglis, arrived in Serbia in 1915, they found that the people doubted their medical skills. Soon the people's attitudes were changed by the efficiency and kindness with which the women performed their medical work. In Evelina's case, her acceptance was enhanced by her excellent ability to ride cavalry horses. She had enjoyed riding from childhood and soon became part of the elite Serbian horse riders, although not a member of the army.

After the Serbian army retreated from Serbia, Evelina became commander of the SWH transport team which went to Russia. The women cut their hair short and wore sharp looking uniforms. Their task was to drive into the areas of fighting and find and transport the wounded and exhausted soldiers back to the hospital. She received a medal from Russia for these endeavors. The SWH teams left when the Russian Revolution was increasing the dangers of the situation, and they returned to England. This did not deter Evelina from continuing her war relief work in England, and she joined Flora Sandes in creating a fund for Serbian soldiers and prisoners.

After the war ended, Evelina returned to Serbia to assist in establishing an orphanage for many Serbian children who lost one or both parents in the war. The site selected was in the mountain range of Bajna Basta, a place of great poverty and with many memorials to soldiers who died in the Drina River campaign. In 1920, however, she contracted pneumonia and died at age 52 in the town.

The gratitude of the Serbian people continues on to present times to this English woman who served them courageously. In 2014 a new plaque dedicated to Evelina was placed at the museum containing her memorabilia. She was buried at Bajna Basta with full military honors. The town was closed down to honor her burial, and it was said the entire population attended out of love and respect for this Englishwoman who gave her life to help them through the terribly difficult war time.

Flora Sandes
The English Woman Who Joined the Serbian Army

Flora Sandes

Flora achieved fame from the time she, an English woman, enlisted in the Serbian army in 1914. She was 38 years old and had lived the life of a respectable lady until she decided to travel around the world. It was said she once shot a man in self-defense while in America. From her early age, it was apparent she wanted excitement and adventure, and the opportunity to enlist as a private in the Serbian army was too tempting to resist. Serbia was one of the few armies that allowed women to fight in combat. Before enlisting, she worked briefly with an ambulance service, which was sent to Serbia only eight days after its formation.

On the front lines, Flora fought bravely, risking her life for others, and rapidly rose to the rank of Sergeant-major. However, she shared more than fighting with the men. She liked racing cars, smoking, drinking, and other masculine pursuits. In one hand-to-hand fight, she was severely wounded by shrapnel, and a lieutenant risked his life to pull her to safety. The severity of her wounds did not deter her, and when she was healthy enough, she returned to the front. She even survived a case of the "Spanish flu." For her actions, she received many medals.

Returning to civilian life was difficult for Flora. She met and married Yuri Yudenitch, a "white Russian" officer in 1927. But political problems and the German invasion in 1941 made their marriage difficult, and Yuri died that year. Flora was not afraid of the Nazis and once again, at age 65, she wore a uniform and served in the Yugoslavian army. However, she was captured and questioned by the Gestapo and had to report regularly to their office. Once the war ended, she decided to travel to Jerusalem, where she lived with her nephew. In her later years, her biggest thrill was to attend the annual reunion of the Salonika Association, where she could count on being treated as the heroine she was.

She lived her last years in Suffolk, England, where she died at age 80. History records her as a woman ahead of her time, one who showed the world what a capable and courageous woman could accomplish.

PART SIX

STORIES OF COURAGE

IT WAS GOD'S GIFT

An Interview with Lazar Jovanovic by the Author

Bozidar Jovanovic was 16 when he was jailed by the Austrian-Hungarian soldiers in 1914 soon after the assassination of the Archduke Ferdinand of Austria in the city of Sarajevo. Bozidar was jailed not for any law he had broken, but he was of Serbian nationality, and Serbians were under suspicion because of the murder of the future emperor. The assailant was of Bosnian nationality but was part of an underground terrorist group operating out of Serbia. That meant that many Serbs living and studying in the Hungarian portion of the empire were jailed or fled the area.

Bozidar spent a year in an Austrian prison before the International Red Cross obtained his release. His young age was an important consideration in gaining his freedom. His story is told by his eldest son, Lazar Jovanovic, a resident of Kansas City, Kansas.

Somehow, Bozidar safely returned to his home in Belgrade, Serbia, although by this time, Serbia and Austria-Hungary were at war. He located some Serbian soldiers who took him under their protection. Because he was under the military age of 18, he could not officially join the army. It was about this time that the Vojvoda Putnik made the difficult decision that his army must retreat from Serbia because of the shortage of troops and ammunition. The expected supplies from the Allies had not arrived and would not. Although the Serbs suspected this, they were not officially notified. Thus began the historic Great Retreat of Winter 1915.

There were about 225,000 soldiers in the retreating army. Along the way the soldiers were ordered to conscript all boys over 12 years old in the villages. This totaled 20,000 to 30,000 youths. The exact number is unknown. This conscription was to prevent them from being seized by the Germans to be used as forced labor in camps where they often starved to death. The Germans were also known to require the older boys to wear a German uniform and fight with their troops. Accompanying the Retreat were unknown numbers of peasants, thousands certainly. They fled their homes and abandoned their farms, which the enemy burned and destroyed. Sometimes the family was trapped inside as the cottage was burned. Many of those who escaped brought their belongings in an ox cart pulled by two to four oxen and their flocks of pigs and sheep. The animals were essential later on as a source of food when the animals themselves became too weak from lack of food and died. The families shared with their neighbors and many of the boys when they had to butcher an animal.

The last group of refugees were the members of the English medical teams, including the Scottish Women's Hospital. They set up temporary hospitals and ten permanent hospitals along the line of retreat, tending to the medical needs of civilians as well as the wounded soldiers. Protecting the rear section of the Retreat were the last line of Serbian soldiers. They often engaged in skirmishes or rear guard actions, adding the new casualties to the wounded from previous battles. The battle sites and times were carefully selected by General Putnik, who gauged the terrain, the number of soldiers available, and the supply of ammunition before he gave orders to fight.

Of this group of perhaps 300,000 or more, only about half survived. At one place before reaching the path to cross the Albanian mountains, the family story is that Bozidar was discovered by his older brother, Bogoljub, who was seated on a horse. Seeing the pitiful condition of his younger brother, Bogoljub gave him a pair of boots and warm clothing.

"This saved my life," Bozidar gratefully said. For weeks he and the others had slogged their way through weeks of rain and mud. Their clothing was in shreds by now and most men had lost or worn out their boots and went barefoot or wrapped their feet in rags or corn shucks. The Serbs wore an unusual shoe made of pigskin called an *opanki*. In good weather it was stuffed with hay or worn with thick handknitted socks and was comfortable. Its toe curved up to make it easier for them to climb the hills and mountains of many regions.

The hero of the story, Bozidar, is on the right; in the center is Miodrag, a brother; and left is Bogoljub, an older brother. All three men served in the army. *Photo of the brothers by Nancy Cramer, courtesy Lazar Johanovic.*

The worst of the Retreat was still ahead of them. When they reached the Kosovo Plain in early November, they were caught in one of the most violent snowstorms in memory. The deep snow was not only difficult to walk through, but it prevented both the people and animals from foraging for food, as they had done in the pleasant fall weather.

The food supply had long been exhausted, and before the snow began, the army trucks brought daily rations of one kilo of bread per soldier. This bread was the only food the army could provide their soldiers, with little or none left for the peasants. The trucks could not drive through the deep snow or risk being trapped in the deep muddy ruts made by the oxen. Some survivors told of going without food for up to seven days, eating the snow to keep hydrated and alive.

Although the army had confiscated the peasants' oxen to pull their artillery, they had to begin to abandon and destroy the guns. Close behind the retreating long line of Serbs, the Germans, whose guns were heavier, had the same problem. The Germans realized that once the Serbs started up the unfamiliar paths into the mountains, it would become difficult, if not impossible, to follow them. Safety for the Serbs lay in the mountains.

A week or more was required to cross the treacherous Albanian mountains. The travelers had gone for days without food or even finding a place in the snow where they could sleep a few hours. The sudden appearance of the dreaded Albanians, who knew the mountain paths, would surprise and frighten the peasants and other civilians. The Albanians were still angry that the Serbs in 1913 had taken over their country in the Second Balkan war, even though the chief powers of Europe nullified that condition of surrender, and the land was restored to the Albanians. They still maintained a vengeful mood. Their ruler, Essad Pasha, had issued an order of safe passage for the Serbians, but often the Albanians ignored his order and robbed or murdered the peasants and soldiers.

Allied Ships Await Retreat Survivors

Finally, the first group of survivors of the march arrived at the beaches of Scutari, where Allied ships were waiting. About half of the total number had perished by now, with an even larger percentage of the young boys. The son of the Minister of Education was one who sadly did not survive. Yet later on the island of Corfu, the minister stifled his grief and continued his work to find schools and homes for the youths who lived through the Retreat.

Between 5,000 and 7,000 boys are estimated to have survived the trials of the terrible journey. Starting in Belgrade, as Bozidar had, they had walked more than 400 miles over a period of four months' time. For others who lived farther south, and closer to the mountain passes, the trek took six to eight weeks of walking. And for nearly all, crossing the rugged mountains with narrow or non-existent paths would have taken seven to 10 days. Many nights they could find no cover or shallow caves in which to bed down.

Lazar has a certificate and a medal given to his father and all the soldiers and youths who lived to complete the Retreat. His father, like so many veterans, preferred not to talk about the Retreat. Lazar said the French took his father and most of the boys to France or England, where they were housed and educated during the rest of the war years. His father was sent to Grenoble, France, for a short time where he completed high school.

Bozidar Becomes a Soldier

The surviving soldiers on the island of Corfu, after regaining their health, joined the French and English troops in the Salonika, Greece, war zone to dislodge the Bulgarians from the southern part of Serbia during the years of 1916-1918. By now Bozidar was old enough to wear a uniform and take up a rifle. He was part of the six regiments of Serbs who fought the Bulgarians on wintry grounds and on mountain crags, often taking the most daring or dangerous assignments. The Bulgarians were the first of the Central Powers to surrender in October, 1918. Loss of this ally made the Germans realize it was impossible for them to win the war.

Bozidar later returned to France, attended a university and earned his Ph.D. in financial planning. The offer of a position with a Belgrade bank brought him back to his home where he married and raised a family.

In the early 1970's, problems with the Tito dictatorship caused Bozidar and his wife to move to the United States, where their son, Lazar, had come to live in 1965. His brother,

Vojko Jovanovic, in 1969 joined Lazar and the few family members already in the United States. Bozidar died in 1974 and is buried in Libertyville, Illinois. His first name, Bozidar, is traditionally given to a male child every other generation in the Jovanovic family. It means literally "God's gift."

For Bozidar and his descendants, the preservation of his life during the terrible years of the war was indeed "a gift from God."

A MONTENEGRIN SOLDIER FIGHTS FOR YUGOSLAVS TO BECOME ONE STATE

An Interview with Rob Palandacic by Telephone and Mail

Rob's grandfather, Luka Palandacic, was only 14 years old and riding his father's horse when the Austrian Sergeant seized him and took him to a nearby Austrian military camp. This was in the small country of Montenegro in a village high in the mountains. The Montenegrins were allies of Serbia and often fought on their side, as they did in 1914 and 1915 until the Serbian army left Serbia. Luka's family had a home in Kotor, a beautiful Montenegrin city on the coast of the Adriatic Sea, and another home in the mountains where they lived for six months a year. They had lived like this for more than 60 years.

Rob's great-grandmother, named Paraskeva, had come from a Russian colony near a free port called Sulina on the Black Sea, which was part of the Ottoman Empire. She married Rade Palandacic, who lived near the Adriatic Sea on the western coast of Montenegro before the Russo-Turkish War of 1877. Rade probably had an opportunity to work at this free port because of the commercial ties between Venice and Kotor, which had a beautiful bay. At the port of Sulina, merchandise from the eastern part of the Black Sea Coast, such as Persian carpets, were imported into Romania, Hungary, and even Austria. Paraskeva was only 17 when she married Rade. She bore him eight children during their marriage. The last child, a boy named Luka, was born when she was 46 years old.

Three of their sons moved to America before World War I began, but Luka stayed in Montenegro because of his young age. Many men from Kotor, which was then part of the Austrian empire, served in the Austrian army, either as volunteers or conscripts. An older brother, Joko, was almost 24 when the war began and would have been wearing the Austrian uniform. He was wounded in probably June 1917. He recovered quickly due to the availability of good medical services for Austrian troops then. He would have been in either the infantry or artillery, Rob is not sure. Luka is believed to have participated in the campaign of the Piave River in Italy, where casualties were extremely high.

Luka's story, fits into a larger narrative about the creation of the Kingdom of Serbs, Croats and Slovenes in 1919 by the Great Powers. However, Rob claimed his grandfather's family were not politically radical. They were satisfied to be ruled by Austria-Hungary. They had lived in Kotor for 60 years, and life was good there. During World War I, Luka served much of his time fighting on the Italian/Croatian front. The Italians never occupied Croatia due to the success of the largely ethnic Croatian army led by Field Marshall Boroevic. Luka also fought briefly in the western part of Slovenia in the aftermath of the war. As one of the victorious Allied armies, Italy was disappointed when their territorial claims around the Adriatic Coast were not granted in the postwar peace conference.

In conducting the Italian campaign, the Croat/Bosnian forces which included Luka's unit, were basically preparing to proclaim a postwar united Yugoslavia. This union would be of critical importance to the various countries involved. King Petar and other Serbian leaders had long yearned for and fought for a union of the various countries surrounding Serbia. It would be the old Serbian empire, renamed the Kingdom of the Serbs, Croats, and Slovenes. It actually came to fruition in 1919 by terms set by the Allies, but the kingdom only lasted a few years due to internal disagreements.

The high level of economic development in Slovenia, a country north of Serbia, was certainly a "war prize" for the new Yugoslavian Karadjordevic monarchy. The potential union was achieved in part by the blood of those troops, including Luka Palandacic, who defended the territory from the Italians.

The Salonika campaign against the Bulgarians, however, was particularly brutal. The high mountain range, Sokol and neighboring peaks, were so steep that scaling ladders had to be used in the final desperate charges.* Three Serbian divisions, the 122nd, the Sumadija, and the Reserves, conquered Sokol, Koziak, and the other peaks that the Bulgarians had earlier successfully defended for three years against British and French attempts to seize.

The Serbian attacks were reminiscent of the campaign 550 years earlier in the mid 1300's waged by "Stephen Dusan the Mighty," ruler of Serbia. He had been victorious in these mountains. Before the battles of 1917 began, the priests reminded the Serbian soldiers of this great event and called on them to honor Stephen with their own victory in 1918.

*(Author's Note: The family has a postcard from Monastir in this area, possibly indicating that Luka was in one of the six Serbian divisions that defeated the Bulgarians. They are seeking confirmation of this attachment and would be grateful to hear from anyone with information. Send any news to this book's author, and it will be passed on.)

THE POWER OF THE HUMAN SPIRIT
An Interview with Bisevac Blagonic as interpreted by Branko Bosilov, Guide

Bisevac Blagonic, an historian from Kraljevo, Serbia, tells the story about his grandfather's ordeal while escaping the various Central Powers armies in the winter of 1915. This tale involves such unimaginable hardships, one asks what power resides in the human spirit to stay alive during times of extreme suffering.

His grandfather, Blazo Bisevac, was only 22 when he enlisted with three of his brothers in the Serbian army. Another brother was rejected because he was crippled. Their father, more than 45 years old, heard his ban also was called up. He was in the third ban. The third ban meant that his father had military experience and was more than 45 years of age. The third ban was called only after the first and second bans had conscripted all possible men. These older men usually were assigned to communication duties but sometimes had to defend the rear lines. This was according to the laws of the third ban and the conscription rules. The other soldiers in the first and second bans were evacuated first in a retreat. The third ban had to defend the rear of the retreating soldiers and often meant certain death for them. This would include Bisevac's grandfather, but he would be proud to die by defending his country in this duty.

The Bisevac men and others in their division suffered unimaginable deprivations. One of the most difficult times happened when they were crossing the plains of Kosovo. The heavy constant rain turned into one of the worst blizzards in recorded Serbian history. Totally unprepared for the snow and ice, hundreds of soldiers and refugees died of exposure and starvation. Bisevac says his grandfather went seven days without food while shuffling through the knee high snow. The men wrapped themselves in blankets to keep warm. Before the snow started, they had stuffed the cloth wrappings that served as shoes with dry grass. Stopping to search for food or even to sleep meant certain death, so they trudged on. They had some beeswax which they chewed. Some found some raw ears of corn which they ate. Afterwards they suffered intestinal problems from the raw corn.

Weather Affected German Movement Also

But the weather conditions also brought a halt to the advancement of the German artillery. Although their troops had winter clothing and enough food, the difficulty of marching through several feet of snow slowed them down. They were still many kilometers away from the Serbian soldiers and peasants, who moved at a snail's pace.

The Serbs had been assigned to military units by the location of where they lived. Men who lived on one side of a mountain went to a certain unit, men on the other side went to another unit. In small towns like Krajlevo, located in central Serbia, all their troops were assigned to the famed Sumadija unit. Though this would seem a practical plan, having men together who knew each other, when an artillery shell wiped out a gun crew, or a machine gun dealt disaster to a squad, the loss was unbearable for the community.

A local monument is engraved with some of the places where the Sumadija unit fought, including Bitola, Skoplje, and Kumanovo. The memorial honors the soldiers who served in 1912-1918. Serbia and other Balkan countries had fought each other in 1912 and 1913 before being invaded by Austria in 1914. This is perhaps where Blazo became an experienced soldier.

No Food or Shelter to be Found

After leaving Kosovo behind them, the men were ordered to take the treacherous winding route to Scutari to find food in Andrijevica along the way, but the food stored in the military magazines there had been emptied. There was no food to be found anywhere. Discouraged but determined, they walked to Podgorica, the location of another magazine. Again, the magazine was empty. Almost faint from hunger and weeping with disappointment, some men left and tried to find a trail that would lead to their homes. Most of them probably either froze or starved to death, as they were many kilometers from they where they lived. However, despite the urging of their comrades to stay, they left. It would seem improper to call them "deserters," as King Petar when announcing the Retreat dissolved the oath of allegiance all soldiers had taken to him and Serbia, thus freeing them to leave the army rather than undertake the rigors and unknowns of the Retreat.

Gathering what little courage they had left, and calling upon the bonds of brotherhood, as was typical of Serbs, the remainder struggled on to Scutari. There they found medical help and some food. But the anticipated ships were no longer there. The Soldiers were too late. The ships had departed several days before with soldiers and civilians who had arrived earlier. The Soldiers had preference over male civilians but women and children were allowed to fill remaining space on the rest of the ships.

Because the Germans had knowledge of this escape plan, the Adriatic was filled with waiting submarines. The Italian ship crews risked their lives on this mission. In addition, the ships could not stay in port for long periods because Austrian airplanes attacked them. The diving planes fired machine guns and dropped bombs on the helpless people on the beaches. The people sought what shelter was offered by the piers and nearby trees and buildings, but it was insufficient coverage for most. There were many dead bodies of soldiers and civilians littering the beaches.

The only alternative left to the downcast remnants of troops and civilians was to rest a few days in a safe place away from the beach and then stagger down the coast to Valore more than 100 kilometers away (about 65 miles). Somehow, most of them made the long journey, where they found Greek Red Cross workers who gave them food and clothing. The English medical staff tended to their wounds and frostbite. They were fed broth or water, if the broth was gone, as their starved stomachs could not handle regular food at first.

French Ships Arrive at Valore

When the French ships arrived a few days later at Valore, Albania, the French sailors helped the Serbians into small boats and rowed them to the ships. When one ship was filled to capacity, it immediately left the harbor, sailing in a zigzag pattern to lessen its chances of being sunk by the lurking German submarines.

Bisevic says his grandfather, always a man of slight build, weighed only 36 kilos or 79.3 pounds when rescued. But the grandfather regained his strength and health in only 17 days, at which time he was deemed healthy enough to return to active duty. (As with many stories these numbers are retold many times, and it is difficult to verify them.)

The soldiers were taken to the Greek island of Corfu, where they were nursed back to health and began training with the new French weapons provided for them. The men were given new French army uniforms and supplies. As a way of honoring their courage, they were allowed to wear the traditional "*sajkaca*" Serbian cap.

After becoming skillful using the new French weapons, they boarded ships at Corfu and sailed to the port of Salonika. From there they traveled overland to the northern part of Greece, where they, along side the French and British forces, renewed the fight against the Bulgarians. This area is near the southern border of Serbia. The Serbs began to achieve significant victories. The combined French and English armies had fought a futile two- year campaign, the "Salonika campaign." They had made no progress because of the epidemic like episodes of malaria, sending hundreds of Allied soldiers home, too ill from repeated bouts of malaria to fight. The war had come to a stalemate until the Serbs arrived with the determination to regain this part of their homeland.

However, in 1916, with the influx of six regiments of Serbs who were renewed in health and purpose, the fighting took on an intensity not seen before. Rugged plains, scattered with huge boulders and caves which the Bulgarians had heavily fortified, presented challenges for the attacking Serbs. They also had to scale the formidable mountains where they captured the well hidden Bulgarian machine gun nests. Artillery was hauled up by rope, as in the Italian mountain campaign. The Serbs fought the Bulgarian troops in merciless attacks, taking revenge for the stories they had heard from home of atrocities. The outrages included rape and torture; the hanging of men, even the priests; and crucifying women.

Bisevac said when his grandfather returned home, he was 26 years old. None of the men in the family had been wounded or injured, an amazing fact. One brother was taken prisoner by the Hungarians and held three years. Family legend tells that his experience with war was entirely different. He was handsome and well-built and found favor with lonely Hungarian women. At least so the story goes.

As for Blazo, he married Stana a few years later. They had only one child, a daughter who died. Bisevac proudly displayed a photograph of Stana and Blazo. The war never ended for Blazo, despite peace treaties and words of assurance from the new King Alexander. He experienced terrible nightmares about his ordeal during the snowstorm and crossing the icy Drina River. He recalled scenes of animals and men drowning in its cold swift flowing waters. Blazo kept seeing images of his comrades sicken or die from the enemy's bullet. He had almost starved to death. His hardships showed on his face in the photograph. He was only 58 when he died. He was a man who suffered without reprieve during all his adult life. He was but one of hundreds of Serbian soldiers who had the strength of spirit and body to survive their challenges.

He returned home, but his mind could never forget those trials. They haunted him to his last day.

CHOOSING LIFE OR HONOR
The Czech Legions – Interview with Milos Hrvolk by e-mail

The 16-year-old boy had one of two difficult choices to make, and one of them could be dangerous. He had been conscripted by the Austrian-Hungarian army and was fighting the Russians. The safe choice to make would be to continue fighting with the Austrians. But the Russians were his brothers; they were fellow Slavs. How could he keep on killing his kinsmen? This was the decision confronting the great uncle of Milos Hrvolk during World War I. The great uncle was in Italy when the Italians finally won an important and bloody victory over the mighty army of the Austria-Hungary Empire. Milos tells what he remembers of his great uncle's dilemma.

The first name of Milos's great uncle has been lost, but his surname was Brnwkovic. How he happened to be captured is also a missing story. Years before, his family had been forcibly moved from Slovakia to Austria by the Austrian-Hungarians along with hundreds of other Slovak families as a way to eliminate the barrier of religion. The families were forced to give up their Orthodox form of religion and convert to the Catholicism practiced by the empire. Also, they were good farmers, and the empire needed more production of food.

Once World War I began, young boys near the military age of 18 were at constant risk of being conscripted. They were seized from the fields or taken while walking on the roads with no adult men to protect them. The boys usually had no opportunity to say goodbye to their family, so families never knew exactly what had happened to their sons.

They helplessly assumed the boys had been conscripted. (It was during these years that a great number of Slavs and Hungarians emigrated to America.)

While Milos's great uncle served with the Austrians, he always was looking for an opportunity to escape. His chance finally came after the battle the Austrians lost to the Italians at the River Piave during June 15-23, 1918. The Italians won a decisive victory, taking many Austrian prisoners and killing or wounding thousands. This was when Milos's great uncle, along with other Slovak soldiers, made their escape to a nearby Russian Czarist unit.

The battle was a huge loss with a total of 150,000 soldiers from both sides killed or wounded. Many Austrians drowned trying to cross the river to escape the Italian guns. The river was called "Bloody River" because the blood of hundreds of dead soldiers filled it for several miles. Normally the water was brown in color, but this disaster meant the red colored river kept its new name for years, according to family stories.

Young man, name unknown, is honored in the Mausoleum of the Zejtinlik Cemetery in Thessaloniki. Many of his young age fought because of the high death rate and shortage of men for the Serbian army. *Photo by Nancy Cramer.*

The Slovaks who had escaped conscription, along with men from the countries of Czech and Slovenia, formed their own units elsewhere and joined the Allies' side. It is believed the great uncle joined one of these units. The Czechs wanted to gain independence for Moravia and Bohemia in the Austrian Empire. The Slovaks and Slovenes desired freedom from the domination of the Hungarians.

Serbians Reinforced by Volunteers Locally and Abroad

Volunteers, both Czechs and Slovenes and those from other places, formed small armed guerilla units in 1914. Some escaped from Austrian captivity and joined nearby Russian units, who were also fighting the Austrians. They ended up with an army of about 40,000 men. In 1917 they became known as the Czech Legions and participated in the Russian civil war, siding with troops loyal to the czar or the White Army. They fought his opponents, known as the Bolsheviks or Red Army.

The Bolsheviks, who had taken over the Russian government in October 1917, a few months later signed the Brest-Litvosk Treaty with the Germans. Later on July 17, 1918, the Bolsheviks executed the czar and his family. But the Czech Legions continued fighting the Bolsheviks farther east into Siberia and north near Archangel when they finally disbanded in 1920 and returned home.

Milos' great uncle was wounded somewhere in the fighting and died. His family learned of his death but never learned the exact circumstances. They did know he had made a courageous attempt to save his honor when he defected from the Austrians. If he had been caught, he would likely have been shot immediately. It was a brave decision for a 16-year-old-boy to make. He chose to defend his Slavic brothers, and this made his family proud.

BACKBONE OF THE SUMADIJA ARMY
Interview With Bosilka Stevanovic, Serbian guide

Photo courtesy of Bosiljka Stevanovic, a Serbian guide, of her grandfather, Aleksander Radojwic, featured in this story.

It was large families like the Radojevics, who, when Serbia called, answered the call without question. They cleaned their rifles, packed a knapsack, and wore their warmest clothes if they had no old uniforms. Then they joined their unit when it passed by their farmhouse or mountain cottage. All the men on one side of the mountain joined the same division. In this case it was the Sumadija, named after a large forest nearby.

This particular family sent Aleksander and his five brothers. They left their families behind in the small village of Ivanjca, where other relatives lived and could take care of each other. The farming was left to the old men and the young boys; consequently the harvests were poor and Serbians in many places almost faced starvation. Various members of the Radojevic family had engaged in a lucrative import-export business, but they took up their rifles to serve their country.

After months of fighting, the Sumadija Division gained honors for its valor, but now the Germans and Austrians were closing in on the small Serbian army that remained. Voyoda Putkin declared that the army should retreat over the Albanian mountains. They would never surrender to the Central Powers. The Radojevic brothers all survived the Retreat and went to Salonika in 1916 to continue fighting. In later years, one brother, Milan, became a diplomat and worked in different Yugoslav Embassies until the start of World War II. His job was made difficult by pressures from the Communists. Bosiljka describes it, saying, "The Communists made his life hell in other ways," although he was not killed, but many others who were not in favor of Tito's government were killed.

Another brother, Antonije, was a mechanical engineer by profession and after World War I ended, he was appointed the Minister of Transportation under Prime Minister Pasic. It was stated that during his tenure the trains actually ran on time. In his position, he was reputed to be the only minister that did not become rich. Unfortunately, Aleksander was executed by the Communists in 1944 for participating in an opposition group.

In her early years as a small child, Bosijka listened to Grandfather Aleksander repeat the story of the Retreat over and over. On winter nights, he peeled apples, telling it word for word the same way. Sometimes her mother would scold Grandfather for telling the story they had heard hundreds of times, but he was deaf to her words. He could hear only his voice reciting the tragic story of when he and his brothers made the Retreat and survived. Bosiljka recalls,"I remember him being loving and caring for my sister and me. His lap was the most comfortable and comforting place for us."

She adds, "That scene printed indelibly of the old Grandfather, peeling apples and reciting his story from memory, will go to the grave with me."

Antonije-Anta Radojevic served in the Serbian army. He had a degree in engineering. *Photo courtesy, Bosiljka Stevanovic, his great-niece.*

Two of the Radojevic brothers. Names unknown. *Courtesy Bosiljka Stevanovic.*

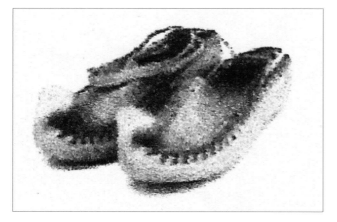

These are the boots that most Serbian soldiers had to wear. They are called *"opankis"* and are made from pigskin. The upturned toe makes it easier for the wearer to climb hill or mountain sides, but the material is delicate and wears out easily. Many men had to resort to using strips of cloth filled with grass or straw when they could not get boots or *opankis*. *Public Domain.*

PART SEVEN

HISTORIC RETREAT BEGINS

THE DECISION IS MADE

For the Serbs, the situation was desperate and more importantly, it seemed hopeless. The troops of the three enemies had begun an encirclement of the Serbian troops. The latter had only a few hundred square kilometers (less than 100 square miles) under their control and less than two weeks of supplies. London correspondent Gordon-Smith wrote, "Ten days would see the last cartridge fired." Lack of forage for the animals doomed a hundred thousand animals to starvation. "The cause of Serbia was lost," Gordon-Smith concluded in his writings.

On November 24, 1915, a government council considered all its options. Deciding the options were few but that surrender was not one of them, a decision was made. The army would evacuate Serbia by retreating over the Kora and Prokletije mountain ranges of Albania. In ports on the Adriatic Sea, Allied ships would rescue the soldiers and refugees. Ironically, the name "Prokletije" means "Accursed Mountains" in Serbian.

Other Reasons Not to Surrender

Several facts determined the decision. First, the Serbs had pledged to the Allies that they would not sign a separate peace treaty with the enemy. Defeated Serbia might be, but not conquered. Second, a surrender meant the dynasty of King Petar would end. He would have to abdicate. Third, the members of the government would be arrested and would probably be exiled for life from Serbia.

On the other hand, the treasury of Serbia had been exhausted by the two Balkan wars, and the rest had been earlier sent abroad. There would be no funds for the royal family, some government officials, and Serbian soldiers. The army was physically and mentally exhausted. It had been depleted by the typhus epidemic earlier that year and by constant fighting. The weather was unpredictable for the oncoming months, and vast amounts of snow could make the march almost impossible. The army would have to destroy all its guns except the small mountain guns. Also to be destroyed were transport wagons, automobiles, and any other vehicle of possible use to the enemy.

Everything that could not be carried on a pack animal also would be destroyed. Because the hooves of horses were not reliable in the mountains, only oxen and mules could be loaded with as much necessities as the animals could carry. The horses would be abandoned, perhaps some bought or stolen by the Albanians, others to starve to death.

There was no time to organize, so the army would travel in small groups rather than in ranks. Actually, this served as an advantage because food and lodging for the night were scare. Sometimes not enough for even a squad, much less a regiment. There were three routes originally planned. One route went to Scutari in Montenegro, another to Durasso (Durres) in Albania, and a third one also to Scutari but by a southern route. The latter route is the one the king and his government officials took. The king, now 71 years old and whose condition of near blindness had caused him to appoint his son as regent that year, rode and walked the entire Retreat, as did his son. Sometimes, the old king drove an ox cart, inspiring the song, "King Petar's Ox Cart," as he drove it to Valona (Valores), about 100 kilometers south of Durazzo. Hapless troops who had arrived too late at the other ports, were forced also to walk the additional length to Durazzo.

When the news was announced to the troops, Gordon-Smith reported, "Grief and bitterness was written on the faces of many (commanders) who had fought five victorious campaigns. They would have preferred to be in the fighting line and… died at the head of their men, rather than have seen this tragic hour." He added the army "had done its duty and more than its duty… her honor at least was intact."

The Soldier, who had listened to the government council's deliberations, shook his head in doubt and disappointment. Yet, what alternatives were there? He knew that with good fortune, most of the army would survive, despite prospects of starvation, injury on the mountains, and bitter temperatures. Those who did not survive would live long in the hearts of their comrades.

Yes, this was the only possible answer to an impossible situation, he decided. He left to rejoin the nearest regiment.

Why The Boys Had to Retreat

The Serbian government decided that all the boys aged 12-17 should be evacuated from Serbia to keep them out of the hands of the enemy. The Germans were known to use young boys in forced labor camps, or if they were old enough to carry a rifle, they became soldiers. But Bulgarians usually killed the boys in revenge because of their long hatred of the Serbs. The Austrians were unpredictable, but the outcome was always brutal.

The Retreat begins with soldiers walking or riding, and peasants and boys walking as they flee the approaching enemy armies. *Public Domain.*

Therefore, leading citizens not already in the army, such as schoolteachers and priests, were assigned a group of 30 to 50 village boys to lead the group on the dangerous but necessary Retreat to what was hoped to be safety. Serbia needed to save a generation of young boys to assure the continuity of their nation.

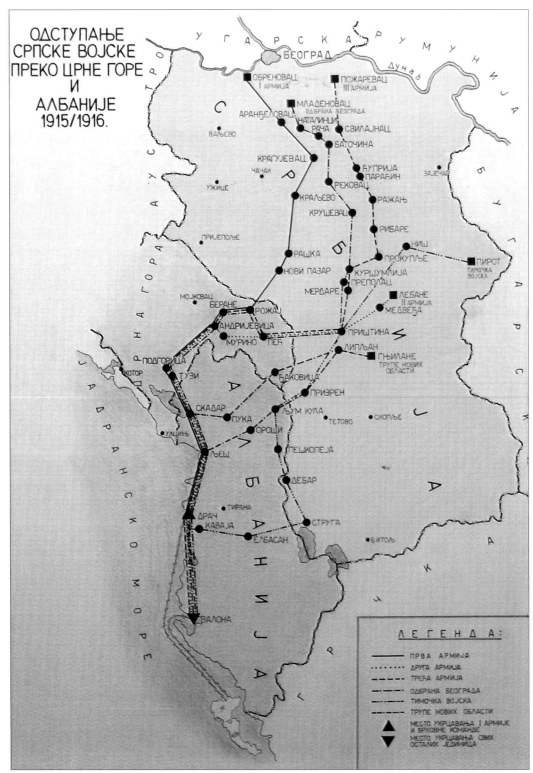

Map shows different routes taken by the Serbs in the Retreat. Names of towns are spelled in Cyrillic alphabet.
Public Domain.

DEVASTATION AND DESTRUCTION
A Story as Envisioned by the Author

The small remnants of a unit in the Drina Division trudged through the late afternoon. Of the original company of 130, there were less than 50 men dragging their exhausted bodies through the grip of a muddy road. Some had dropped out earlier when they reached their villages; others had collapsed by the roadside, unable to walk another kilometer. Some sick soldiers had been rescued by ox carts from a nearby English medical tent hospital. They were taken for treatment of their wounds.

Two soldiers, Mitar and Ljuba, were from the same village. Soon they would reach the nearest farm, that of Ljuba's uncle, where they would stay a while before going to their own homes. If they had any homes left, that is. During their homeward march they had seen the actions of the Bulgarian soldiers who burned houses, tore down fruit trees, and wrecked the contents of the small cottages. They came to the village church, and cried aloud when they saw the burned out interior. Only crumbling walls of sundried brick painted white were left standing. The two men dropped out of the line of soldiers and looked unbelievingly at the wreckage.

It Was as Bad as They Feared

Mitar exclaimed, "The Bulgarians have been here too. I thought they had swung up north. Destroying our church, the blasphemy of them! Let's check out the cemetery," and he climbed the rail fence. Despite his fatigue, he dashed to the cemetery on the other side of the church. Then he wailed, "The graves, my father and grandfather's-all dug up!" and he fell to the ground on the piles of dirt. Ljuba hurried to his side and tried to comfort his friend.

"Come, Mitar, we can rebury the dead tomorrow. It is bad, I know, but we must see your family. We must be sure they are all right." He helped his friend to his feet and gave him a drink of water from his nearly empty skin bag. Mitar straightened his *sajkaca*, (cap) brushed the dirt off his long coat, and followed Ljuba back to the road. They walked nearly a kilometer to the one street of the small village and stopped at the third house. The gate was falling from its post, the thatched roof had great holes from shrapnel, and the grove of protecting trees from western winds, resembled giant match sticks.

Mitar rapped on the door with his rifle butt. A light shone through one of the two windows on the front of the house. The door opened, and his Uncle Milo stood in the doorway. He looked at the two ragged and dirty soldiers, then exclaimed, "Mitar, my boy, come in, come in! You are alive. The Holy Mother be thanked!"

The two soldiers came into the house where they were greeted with hugs and words of welcome. Then Mitar's Aunt Dajana stood back and examined the two men. "A bath and a scrub with my brush, for you two. First something to drink. Will it be hot or cold?" and she winked and pointed at the bottle in the middle of the table.

"This is the real drink," she said. "The Bulgarians took everything in sight. But we had one bottle hidden in the cow shed. It's been standing here once we were told that some of our army was allowed leave to come home. And you're here, my boys! You are here. Let's drink up." She brought out some small glasses—none were matching—and immediately poured some of the fiery rakjia into each.

The men drank up, swallowing the rakjia in one gulp, then followed it with another glassful. Mitar's anger and sadness were beginning to disappear. He was home, and tomorrow they would hear the news. Tonight he and Ljuba would rejoice at being a family again. Ljuba, too, was now family.

The Order of the Day

"We retreat when it's fully dark," Goran whispered to Milomar, the man next to him. "Pass the word down the line, the Sergeant told me to."

Even with the noise of the Austrian Fifth Army's large guns bombarding the trenches, the men from habit still resorted to whispers. "Retreating?" Milomar snorted angrily. "Serbs don't retreat—you know that. They stay and fight to the last man."

Goran impatiently explained, "General Sturm ordered us to leave the trenches. They're too shallow to protect us all night from the barrage of large field guns." During the rest of the war, the Serbs' sudden attacking and retreating tactic proved to be vital to their survival to winter of 1915 when the actual Retreat began.

The men joined the line of the other soldiers, each bending over carrying their heavy kits under one arm, their rifles with the other. The Battle at Belgrade and the Sava River was over for them, once the Austrians crossed back over between Sremska Mitrovica and Sabac. At least these Serbs here could walk away without any help, while too many of their brothers lay dead or wounded on the rocky hillsides. Perhaps the general would counterattack, and then the bodies might be recovered. If not, then the soil of Serbia would claim their bodies and hallow the ground. The soil had been blessed many times during the many uprisings and revolts that Serbia fought during the 1800's, and again, in the Balkan wars of 1912 and 1913.

The Serbs' Third Army regrouped to liberate Sabac, while the rest of the Third Army protected the important town of Valjevo. This and other surprise attacks by the Serbs took advantage of the many swirling rivers, uneven terrain, and stands of trees to shield them. These skirmishes confounded the confident Austrians. At night the Austrians began to pull back secretively beyond the boundaries of Belgrade. Victory belonged to Serbia in 1914.

To Leave the Army or to Stay

Milomar and Goran stepped out of the line of the soldiers. They had seen in a deserted peasant's yard, something they needed. Goran jerked the petticoat off the rope where it had been drying. Then he took his knife and quickly cut the rope off the tree.

"This will make good wrapping for my feet for a while," he explained. "My *opanki*s are in shreds and soon my feet will be bleeding," he told Milomar. "This cloth will last a few days until we get into more mud, then I will go barefoot again."

Not replying, Milomar was searching the ground in the dark for apples dropped from the trees after the peasants had left. His stomach was making noises. How long had it been since the army bread truck had made it to the trenches? Two days ? Three days? He found apples, some with a worm or two. No problem. A couple with bruises proved no obstacle. He just hoped they were ripe enough. Otherwise, the dysentery would slow them down, besides making them miserable. They were in luck. The apples were ripe. He filled his kit and handed the rest to his friends. "We're in good shape now. Let's get back to the line before we're missed. We can always say we had to take a leak."

No charges of desertion would ever be filed against them because the king had released his soldiers from their oath of allegiance to him. A few soldiers missed their families or were desperately needed at home and took a chance on getting a leave, official or unofficial.

The Soldier had been following the two men and felt relieved when they found food and kept to their decision not to be deserters. The men marched several more hours in the darkness before they reached headquarters. A hut with a roof and a dry dirt floor promised a few hours of sleep. The orders tomorrow would be tough.

That year, in 1915, with the mighty German army in charge, events provided an entirely different story. The entrance of Bulgaria on the side of the Central Powers is when tales of real courage and fortitude began.

THE FIRST PART OF THE RETREAT
A Story as Envisioned by the Author

When the two men joined their group, it had started to rain. Goran hid the petticoat and stolen clothesline he had wanted to wrap around his wet head and instead pulled his jacket over his head to make a hood. He grumbled, "Won't do any good to hurry, this road will turn into mud like on the Sava. When the guns get stuck, we'll be the oxen and pull them out."

Milomar added, "There are hardly any shells left. We might as well leave them behind, they're too heavy to carry on our backs." A few disapproved of their complaining.

All were used to hardships before, and these problems were nothing a Serb could not manage. Goran muttered a religious curse and spit.

Milomar, shocked, crossed himself. "Don't be blasphemous! What would Father Cedric say? We're headed for Urize where the Montenegrins will give us food." Milomar tried to reassure his comrade as they approached a road swarming with fleeing villagers.

"Look at all those peasants crowding the road." Ox carts were stuck in the mud or overturned. The giant yoked pairs of oxen heaved to pull themselves from the watery mud. "We'll have to take our artillery around them," and Miramar shouted, "Out of our way."

Snow covered paths and below zero temperatures added to tribulations of the Retreat. *Public Domain****.

A Serbian priest conducts burial rites for massacred *"Komitas"* or Serbian querilla fighters. *Public Domain****.

The peasants, hearing men's voices, turned and stared angrily at the soldiers. An elderly man retorted, "You soldiers think you're so brave! You're supposed to be back at the rear lines protecting us. You're running away, too, and you have rifles and we have nothing," and he looked away in disgust, muttering, "In 1876 against the Turks we didn't have it so good either."

A woman screamed, "Maybe you're deserting us, too! Our army is full of cowards." She began weeping, her head in her hands. Her children, clinging to her wet skirts, started crying too.

Milomar said, "Now look what you've done. We're going to get out of here. Let the Germans have their way with those stupid peasants. They don't know what we've been through. Climbing over stacks of dead bodies in the trenches; wounded filling every store and barn. No hospitals. We're not cowards, but we've got to have guns to fight with. The Allies promise guns, ammunition and food but send us nothing. Nothing but empty words."

The two men found the edge of the road and walked past the clutter of carts, animals, and people. They caught up with their troops. All were exhausted and discouraged.

THE ENGLISH CAPTAIN AND HIS BOYS
A Story as Envisioned by the Author

On a side road near a small village, Captain Edgewick was leading his small band of boys, now reduced to about thirty. Hunger, cold and exhaustion had taken some lives already. Captain Edgewick, a British doctor, suffered physically with the boys, but his suffering also was more of a moral nature. He asked himself how could he possibly lead the boys safely through dangers that constantly threatened their lives. If only he had Major Slbodon to talk to. He would have some answers, but the major was lying in an ox cart somewhere in the line, ill with pneumonia. He might even be dead after this torrent of cold rain.

"Where is common sense? Who made these decisions to retreat? Do they have no concern for the soldiers or the peasants?" He talked on as if another person was walking with him. "The world is crazy. It is ruled by insane men, safe in warm and dry houses, and offices with servants."

"Boys, here's a cave under the rock shelf. It looks dry. I'll build a fire with those sticks near the back. We'll rest and try to warm our clothes, and I'll bring out the cheese I was saving for supper." Some of the boys politely cheered, others just dropped where they stood. They were too cold and numb to feel any relief about resting or eating.

Dragutin and Janko huddled together, sharing the dry jacket Janko had worn under his sheepskin jacket. Dragutin asked, "Will we make it to wherever we're going? Will we ever see our mothers again? I don't believe my mother is still alive. The terrible stories the peasants tell about the enemy hanging women and priests." His voice trembled. He continued, words rushing, "My mother would speak out at the bad things the Germans are doing. She would be the first to make them mad and get into trouble. She may be hanging from a rope right now."

Finally, the warm fire, the piece of cheese and bread the captain carefully measured out for each boy was comforting. Lying close to each other, the two boys fell asleep. The captain looked at his boys, all were sleeping. Maybe this is our end, he wearily thought, and dozed off himself.

THE SCHOOLMASTER LEADS HIS BAND OF BOYS
A Story as Envisioned by the Author

The schoolmaster blew his whistle again. The scuffling boys quickly formed two lines and stood at attention. "Now, when I blow that whistle once, you must get into your lines. No delay. There may be guns aimed at us and it will be important to listen to my words." He paused and looked at his boys. There were two lines of about ten boys each. They ranged in age from 12 to 16 and were dressed in the warmest clothes their mothers could scavenge.

The boys looked straight ahead, except for one small boy on the end. He broke his forward look to glance at the schoolmaster, who caught him. The boy held his breath, hoping the schoolmaster had forgotten where he put his stick. Giving the boy a frown, the schoolmaster continued. "I am responsible for you and your safety from now on. Your families trust me. So you must do exactly what I tell you. I will do my best to get you over the Albanian mountains and to the coast of Albania on the Adriatic Sea. There the French and Italian ships will take us to safety. It will be a hard trip, but you are brave and strong boys. The big ones will help the smaller ones. All of us will help each other, God willing. We have a long walk across Serbia from Nis, our home town. It will be at least 300 to 400 kilometers. (180-240 miles), and also climbing mountains. Now, let us say the prayer for departure."

They all bowed their heads and softly repeated the prayer, then crossed themselves. Most of the boys loved and trusted their schoolmaster. They also wanted him to be proud of their efforts to live up to his expectations. The schoolmaster asked Nikolai to start the song:

Fight to keep your liberty,
Then slavery never fear.
Come, oh come! Serbians arise,
Follow, brothers, follow,
For home and family ties.
Shield the people from disgrace,
And let us bravely die
For Serbia, our Mother dear,
While you hear our battle cry;
Come, oh come, Serbians arise,
Follow, brothers, follow,
For home and family ties.

The Soldier watched as Nikolai's young voice sang the first few notes. The boys picked up their kits and turned to follow the schoolmaster. A mixture of feelings filled the air as the boys' voices rose in song. This would be an adventure for some. Others kept back tears, remembering their mother's last hug. Was the schoolmaster capable of leading them on this long dangerous journey? The schoolmaster himself had his doubts. He had served in the First Balkan War of 1912 and knew the dangers of war. Surely the Virgin Mary would protect him and his little group as the priest had promised.

The Soldier watched them march off, singing gaily, wrapped in colorful scarves their mothers had knitted for them, probably with a prayer in each stitch. The Soldier had a feeling of apprehension. No, he must not think that way. He should feel hopeful about the long march ahead for the schoolmaster and his flock of trusting boys.

THE AMBUSH OF THE PRIEST AND HIS BOYS
A Story as Envisioned by the Author

Everyday on the long walk seemed the same. The priest would wake the boys at daybreak. They would pack up their blankets and wash their faces and hands if there was a nearby stream. If they had any clean clothes, they changed the dirty ones they had worn for days. Then they waited for the priest to assemble them for morning prayers. Afterwards, the younger boys would go to the nearby source of water and fill the pitchers, while the older boys would cut the bread and cheese, or sausage if any remained, into equal parts. They always seemed to be hungry, and the special treats their mothers had given them upon departure had been eaten during the first days despite the priest's warning about saving some of the food.

On this particular day, the younger boys came running back with empty water jars and bad news. "We saw some soldiers in different uniforms climbing the hill. They were still a long way off and couldn't see us because of the ferns on the river bank."

Petra asked, "Father? Could it be the Bulgarians?" They were still close enough to where they had captured the city of Nis. The priest ordered, "Cover your blankets and kits with leaves and branches, and let's hurry out of here. They may be Bulgarians, and if they are, we will be in trouble."

It Was Too Quiet and Peaceful

The boys quickly buried their belongings under boughs and covered them with leaves, then departed from their sleeping place. The priest ordered the small boys to hide under large low pine boughs and told the older boys to climb trees with large branches so that most of them were well concealed. He himself took shelter behind a huge rock.

Soon they heard footsteps in the leaves and some shouting in the distance. Someone blew a whistle and the group turned away, walking in a different direction. The priest waited some time for the sound of their shuffling through the leaves and their talking to disappear. When he thought it was safe, he softly called to the boys and they emerged from their hiding places.

"We are very lucky. Your patron saints were with us today. You see, it can be safe one minute and the next minute, we could have all been captured or even killed. But each of your saints protected us and will keep us safe, if we are careful. You must do what I say. Now, eat what you can and let's be on our way. We'll have to change direction though. Dusan and Borislav, come with me. Let's go see which way to take." The priest and the two older boys walked off, while the rest of the boys nervously ate the little food they had been given. There was no water to drink this time.

The group found an animal path that seemed safe and followed it for several days. One day as they were resting, it seemed too quiet and peaceful for the priest. Just as he was about to get up and walk around, he saw some men wearing white blousy pants come out of the bushes across the small stream. They carried large guns under their arms.

They were the feared Albanians! Pointing their guns at the boys, they yelled, "Halt! Don't move. Put your hands on your heads and don't even think of running away or you will feel the sting of our guns. We have you surrounded." Despite the different language, the boys instinctively guessed what the words meant.

But one of the boys, Rasko, always a daring one, turned to dart away. The Albanian quickly raised his rifle and fired a shot. It hit the boy in the back. Rasko fell on his face and didn't move. Shocked into silence, the boys stood still. Then they heard an ox cart approaching with men yelling. Maybe they could escape now if they ran fast, so several more of the older boys started running. The Albanians killed or wounded each boy who ran. Then the Albanians turned and disappeared back into the dense forests, waiting to see what the boys would do next.

Elio, small and a fast runner, jumped across the stream and saw a huge cypress with wide concealing branches. He crouched low, knowing other boys had followed him. Would they try to hide with him? He held his breath as he heard the Albanians prodding the trees with bayonets. One soldier found a boy and stabbed him. The child screamed in pain as they stabbed him again and again. "That's for your soldiers killing my son last year in the war," the man's voice screeched with anger.

Then they found the priest and shot him again and again. "Now, you won't try to force your religion on us Muslims again, you filthy ugly Orthodox Serbs!" They cut off his hands. Those were the hands that held the chalice of wine and pieces of bread the Muslims had been forced to drink and eat. Otherwise they paid high taxes or were imprisoned. The soldiers ripped the gold cross from his neck. Then the Albanians left, taking what clothes the boys had in their kits and tugging the shoes off their feet. They searched the little dead bodies for medallions or gold chains and snatched them too. One older boy had climbed near the top of a tall tree. His foot slipped. He came wheeling downward and landed on the ground with a thud. Immediately, he was filled with the Albanians' bullets. It was Zeliko's best friend.

Zeliko was shaking with fear. He had quietly climbed the big tree and settled between a branch in the fork of the trunk. Fortunately, the tree had plenty of large leaves that made a protective shield. He was cold, but he was wearing his older brother's coat and wrapped it around his legs. The brother had said when he left for the army that the coat was too heavy and it was summer and did not need his coat, so he had left it behind. Zeliko missed his brother, but he was glad to have the coat. The sounds of the boys in pain from the stabbings gradually stopped, and Zeliko fell asleep. Then he was awakened by the sound of men's voices speaking Serbian. Help was coming. He almost started crying with relief. He would be rescued.

THE TRAGIC MARCH OF 400 MILES LED BY THE BOYS
A Story as Envisioned by the Author

The two boys had just shut up the sheep into the backyard pen and were walking toward Stefan's weathered cottage. There were gaps in the roof where the thatch was missing and the wooden fence was sagging. The boys saw two soldiers going to the front door. Stefan asked, "What do you suppose they want? Pa's gone to war. Last year my two older brothers died of the typhus. That leaves just me. You don't suppose…," Stefan's voice dropped.

"It's probably nothing," Branko tried to sound encouraging. "You're only 15, and the only man around the house, like me. That's what your Ma said when Yoder and Josef died. Don't worry, they probably want some food. Soldiers are always hungry."

The top half of the door finally opened, and Stefan's mother appeared, wiping her forehead with her apron. Wearily she asked, "What do you want? If it's food, there's some soup left from noon. You're welcome to it, then go and leave us alone."

One soldier looked at the other and hesitated. "It's your son, Stefan. We have orders. We need to take him and the other village lads to train them to fight. The Bulgarians are moving quickly toward us from the east. The Germans and Austrians up north will soon cross the Danube River. We've lost a lot of men. Now we must have replacements, and since your boy's nearly 16…"

The woman angrily interrupted, "He turned 15 last St. Dimitri's Day, and I need him to drive the oxen when we harvest soon. My husband's been away nearly five years now-fighting the Turks, then Albanians, and now the Austrians! What am I to do?" She looked ready to cry.

The second soldier softly said, "I'm afraid we have orders to take the oxen, too. You'll be paid for them by the government. There's talk of the Austrians making a breakthrough down the Morava Valley. If that happens, and the Bulgarians take the town of Nis east of here, we'll all be caught in a trap. You civilians, too. You better be thinking about taking your little ones and heading south. You got relatives there?"

"I don't believe you, and you can't have my boy or my oxen. That's all I have left," she began sobbing. "When will this fighting ever end?"

"Mother, let me explain. We must do this to save Serbia. Now may I please come in and explain what we have to do?" She reluctantly opened the bottom half of the door, and the two soldiers disappeared into the small cottage.

An hour later Stefan and Branko started down the road with the soldiers. They wore small packs on their backs and were dressed in their sturdiest boots and warmest clothes. Branko's cottage was next door. It had not taken long for his mother to give her consent, although his father had been killed in the second war with Turkey two years ago. Now she was left with no one old enough to harvest. But she wanted Branko to help defeat the Austrians. The soldiers picked up boys at other village cottages until there were about 50 in the group. They were 12 to 17 years of age. Some boys were talking excitedly, others were silent.

A few of the youngest were still crying from the last hug their grieving mothers gave them. The group walked until dark, then stopped by a hay field ready for mowing. None of the boys had ever left their village before except Petar, who had gone once with his father to Soljeice to buy a bull ox. The soldiers showed them how to put up the tents stored in the cart that Stefan's oxen were pulling.

"I better go take off their yoke and feed and water them," Stefan told the soldier. Branko went with him. Meanwhile the soldiers built a fire and cooked supper for the hungry boys. It was dark now and no one was talking anymore. The excitement was over, and they had not yet realized what was happening to them. They were tired, and after eating, they crawled into their tents and rolled up in their blankets. Most went to sleep immediately, but Stefan and Branko were awake.

Stefan whispered to Branko, "What do you think the soldiers will do with us? I can shoot a gun; my brothers taught me."

Branko answered softly, "I can shoot too, but we don't have any guns. Where do you think we are headed? I'm worried."

Stefan, trying to comfort his friend, said "They are Serbs, and they will take care of us. That's the way it's always been." The boys had to have faith in what the soldiers said, for they had no way of knowing if the soldiers really would take care of them. The soldiers hadn't explained their plans. Finally sleep came.

The next day the skies were blue and clear of clouds. The soldiers lined up the boys and taught them how to march to a count. Stefan remarked, "They said we would get uniforms and our own gun when another unit catches up with us. That would be great."

Branko agreed. "This would make us real soldiers. We might even find your father's unit. Wouldn't that be a surprise!"

Stefan thought about how happy he would be to see Pa. It had been so long since Pa had left, he wondered if Pa would recognize him. He was just a child then. Now, he was almost grown. And how would Pa look? Would he have gray hair? Had he been wounded? Stefan thought of Pa's infrequent letters, only a few each year. Pa didn't have much schooling and couldn't write. He always had someone write his letters for him. Stefan kept his thoughts to himself. It might make Branko sad, now that his father was dead.

The boys marched each day, taking small rest stops. In a few days they would be taught how to hold the Serbian rifle and load it. The soldiers had barely enough ammunition for their own guns, so they couldn't let the boys actually fire the guns. Stefan told the soldiers, "My friend, Branko, and I have been hunting with our old guns, but I bet I could shoot this new one if I had a chance."

The soldier smiled, "Son, you may get a chance before you know it. The nearby mountains are full of deer, wild boar, squirrels, and rabbits." Stefan looked for mountains but saw only flat farm lands. One day they came to a wide road leading from a nearby town. The road was crowded with peasants, their carts piled high with household goods. Two or sometimes four oxen pulled the carts. The many carts and peasants took up most of the narrow curving road. All day the boys were slowed down behind the mass of carts and the pigs and sheep the peasants had brought along.

Four Miserable Months of Walking

As it grew dark the refugees settled into small groups. The peasants found places near the meadows and built small fires with wood from the forests. The boys and their soldiers did the same. Tiny camp fires all over the fields sparkled in the darkness. Stefan thought out loud, "It looks like all the stars in the heavens have dropped to earth. It is so beautiful."

Branko said, "I wonder if our families are somewhere at the end of the line. Do you think we will ever find them?" They both crossed themselves and said a prayer. Stefan reached beneath his wool shirt for the tiny cross his mother had given him when he left. She had worn it as long as he could remember, and there were tears in her eyes as she fastened it on his neck. Reminding him, she said, "You take good care of it, Stefan, and the cross will take care of you. Remember to recite the prayers the priest taught us to say when we have troubles." Stefan could recall her every word and the worried smile on her face.

As Stefan fell asleep, little did he know that he would spend almost four months on the road, walking nearly 400 miles to safety in Albania. Nor could he know that more than 20,000 Serbian boys also were on their way to safety across the Albanian mountains. Most of those nights from now on, as winter grew near, would be cold and miserable. He would remember with sadness the early part of the journey with the glowing starry nights and tiny camp fires dotting the meadows. The boys walked in a southerly direction day after day. Sometimes they had no dinner if the army supply wagons were too far ahead of them. Then they would help the soldiers look for food in the woods. Sometimes when the peasants had to kill a sheep or pig that died from exhaustion or lack of food, they shared the meat with the boys and soldiers.

As the days passed, the peasants and the boys were joined by more villagers fleeing from their homes. Other villagers stayed behind, believing they would be safe from the enemy. The soldiers urged,"You better come along. Germans can be bad to peasants. They'll take your livestock, your food, even your clothing."

But secretly the soldiers knew how small the Serbian army was and how it would be unable to protect all the refugees. The army lacked provisions for its soldiers, much less the peasants. Protecting the peasants would be difficult, maybe impossible. The soldiers had convinced the boys that if they were captured by the enemy, they would be forced to fight against their own people. No Serb would do that.

Then the winter rains started, making the walking miserable. The heavy downpour soaked the boys, and soon their boots were covered with thick mud. The boys kept their packs as dry as possible because they contained their only extra socks and clothing. One day they crossed a river, stepping on big stones in the middle. The stones were slippery and every now and then, a boy would slip and fall into the icy cold water. The others pulled him out, but the boy would shiver from the cold water. The soldiers took extra blankets from the cart and wrapped them around the soaked boys.

The rain finally stopped and Stefan whispered to Branko, "I hope the soldiers have something to cook in the pot. This cold weather makes me hungrier than ever." But there was only a little food for the pot that night and none of the nearby peasants had food from their meager rations to share. Each group had camped wherever they could find a dry spot. The boys tried to sleep, but their empty stomachs kept many awake. Little did they suspect that this would happen night after night for many weeks.

Questions But No Answers

Stefan and Branko worried, "Where was the army supply cart? When would it catch up with us?" They wanted to ask the soldiers but realized the soldiers were worried themselves and talked in hushed voices. The two boys kept their thoughts to themselves. They didn't want the younger boys to know how desperate the situation was becoming. The younger ones might start crying.

Bogdan, an older boy, asked, "Where are the English soldiers? And the French? They promised to send help." He remembered how kind the English and Scottish nurses had been when they came to Serbia last year. The boys asked the soldiers, "Where are the doctors and nurses?" Neither the soldiers nor the boys could know that their Allies, the French and English, had decided the Serbian campaign was hopeless. They would send no military help because the Allies believed that in a few more days the German and Austrian troops would overcome Serbia.

That meant the Serbs would have to surrender. The soldiers suspected this was why the Allies failed to arrive. What the Allies did not understand was that the Serbs would fight to the last man and never surrender. However, the Serbs did not know that the Allies also were fighting desperately for their lives and could not spare men or supplies.

The Serbian Empire had existed for 500 years until conquered by the Ottoman Empire in 1389. It was built on Serbian courage and determination. It would become an empire again, the soldiers were convinced. Prodded by the older boys, Stefan, the next day, asked the Sergeant, "Where are the Allies?"

The old Sergeant, with his bushy beard and mustache, shrugged his shoulders and said, "They're on the way, lad. On the way." But in his own mind, the Sergeant knew the Allies would not come. The Serbs would have to fight by themselves. He knew also that the previous years of constant warfare between Serbia, Turkey and Bulgaria had devastated the supply of Serbian men. That high casualty rate was one reason the boys had been conscripted.

Older men called "*cheecha*" or "Uncle" signed up to fight. They had no uniforms and were often dressed in rags. They suffered from rheumatism and were half starved. But no Serbian man wanted to be told he was too old to fight. The Sergeant and his soldiers were fearful of being trapped by the Bulgarians coming from the east and south, so every man, young or old, who joined the army, was important to their cause.

At times the peasants had food to give to the boys when some of the starving oxen were too weak to walk. The huge beasts lay down in the road, refused to move and died. The peasants had to hitch other oxen to the dying ones to move them off the road.

All this caused more delays in the endless line of people, animals, soldiers and cannons. The roads grew narrower and muddier as the march slowed down almost to a crawl. Still, the long line of people with carts, soldiers and the boys kept heading toward the Albanian mountains.

One morning the boys heard news that terrified them. The kindly Sergeant said, "Boys, we received important orders last night. We have to return at once to join the rear guard."

The boys had suspicions this might happen, and they had dreaded the news. They could hear the roar of the Germans' big guns in the distance. This meant the Germans and Austrians were trying to break through the Serbian rear line.

The Sergeant added, "Our rear guard must hold the line and block the German advance. Then the retreating soldiers and peasants can make it safely to Albania." Shocked by the news, the boys also knew the Albanians could be dangerous. Just a few years ago in a brutal war with them the Serbs had won. What would the Albanians do to the retreating Serbian soldiers? Or the refugees and the boys? The Albanians were also famous as horse thieves and murderers of strangers.

"What will we do now?" the smaller boys asked. They looked at Stefan and Branko and the bigger boys for an answer. Stefan and Branko looked at each other, fear in their eyes. The Sergeant hurried to say, "Just follow the peasants to the big Prokletijc mountains on the border of Albania. On the other side you will be safe. I'm sorry we don't have much food to leave, but maybe another rear guard army unit will come with food."

He explained apologetically, "We can't leave a gun for you to kill animals for food. You can search the fields for potatoes and Indian corn. The peasants have been generous and feel sorry for you. Many of them have children about your ages. You will be all right."

Patting the heads of some of the smaller boys, with a wave of his hand and a sad look on his face, the Sergeant hurriedly joined the other soldiers. Shouldering their rifles, the soldiers waved goodbye, then turned their backs on the boys. The men quickly marched to the north.

Can We Find the Path to Safety by Ourselves?

Stefan and Branko tried to hide their fears from the smaller boys. They asked Petar and Brogan, "What else can we do?" They would have to follow the peasants and villagers as long as they could. Surely those adults would lead them to safety.

"The Sergeant said safety was just over the mountains, but where were the mountains? All I still see is the green Morova Valley ahead," Stefan commented. "There are a lot of farms, maybe they have some extra food." So the boys started down the road, walking, not marching, to save their strength. Week after week the boys followed the peasants and ox carts. That line was becoming smaller as some families stopped off at villages with people they knew or if they became too weak. At night if the boys couldn't find food in the fields, they sent the younger boys to different campfires to beg for food. The little ones always came back with bread or a piece of cheese or meat to share. The nearby streams provided clear water to drink.

The peasants had been ordered to cut their carts in half and leave some possessions behind. This allowed the line to move faster. No one knew how close the enemy was. It was necessary to keep moving the line to the safety of the mountains. But the responsibility of leading the group of boys was an adult responsibility. The few older boys would have to be the adults now. They didn't know if they could lead the boys to safety.

Then one morning, unexpectedly, a terrible blizzard blew in. The boys put on all their clothes, but were still cold. They had to keep walking or they would freeze. The ghostly figures of peasants wrapped in blankets appeared ahead of them in the blinding snow. Everyone kept walking all day. No one stopped, the snow was too deep now. For the smaller boys it was up to their knees. The older boys had to pull them through the snowdrifts.

The boys found protection under the wide branches of the trees. They huddled together, wrapped in blankets. But for some of the younger boys, the walking, the deep snow, and lack of food was too much. They refused to get up the next morning. They acted like the starved and exhausted oxen who were dying.

Stefan said, "I can carry Zoran on my back," and picked up the small boy. Branko and some older boys tried to carry other little boys, but the snow was too deep. With the extra weight, the older boys kept falling. Stopping, the boys finally realized that each boy had to walk on his own. They had tried to rescue the little ones, but it was too difficult. By now some of the boys' bodies were nearly frozen. Death was near.

Stefan, Branko and Petar found some deep crevices in rocks with spaces big enough for the small bodies. They covered the bodies with pine branches and rocks. The boys each said a prayer and crossed themselves. One boy had some paper and a pencil. He wrote down their names and village. Serbs were used to seeing people dying. It was common in the villages. Older people, babies a few days old, the many who fell to the typhus last year. Even the fathers and older brothers continue fighting miles away in the mountains and near unfamiliar rivers. But these little boys dying was different. It was as if a part of each surviving boy had died also.

At Last, Food, Shelter and Rest

There had always been an adult to lean on and to provide comfort. Now they had only each other. Stefan looked at Branko, knowing he was feeling the same. The boys wrapped their arms around each other and softly sobbed. They were interrupted by a younger boy who had fallen down and hit his elbow against a log. He was crying and others gathered around him to try to comfort him. Branko and Stefan gave each other a last hug and walked over to the small one, hoping the others would not start crying now.

Fortunately the snow stopped. The air cleared and they saw the outlines of a village. There they found food and shelter and rested a few days. There were no longer 50 boys in the group. Several more died the day after they entered the village. Some of the villagers took pity on the smallest boys and offered to keep them in their homes and nurse them back to health. They were still grieving for the little ones they had lost to the typhus last year.

But when Stefan asked, "Do you know where the enemy is?" the villagers had no information. Even reports from occasional soldiers coming from the north were confusing. No one knew how close the enemy was. They would have been terrified if they had known that the Germans were sometimes only a few miles in the rear. But the snow and cold temperatures had affected the Germans' movement also, and they finally had to abandon their bigger guns.

The remaining boys pushed on with their long journey through Serbia. By now the group of peasants was smaller each day. Some of the older peasants sat down on big rocks by the road side and waited until death from hunger or cold overtook them. They looked peaceful sitting there, waiting to die. The boys were sad but they could do nothing to help them.

Bogdan several times wondered, "Will any of us live to make it to Albania?" This angered Stefan who always replied, "Of course, we will make it. We have to. Then we can fight for Serbia and afterwards find our families. Of course, we will!" But even as he said it, he only half believed it was possible.

The Albanian Mountains Finally Appear

Finally the day came when the boys saw the mountain range in the distance. Though they walked each day in that direction, the mountains never seemed any closer. Their hopes rose when they met villagers who pointed out a path that led up and over the 7,000 feet high mountains. The boys gave a weak smile and crossed themselves in gratitude.

Stefan and Branko looked at the mountain peaks with awe. They were so high and steep. How could they possibly climb those mountains? Again, they had no choice. The boys found supplies from the carts and packs of peasants who had died by the road. At first, they were hesitant to take the food and clothing.

Petar said, "If we don't take some food and clothing, you know what will happen to us."

Stefan spoke up, "I think the peasants would want us to save ourselves. Look how many of them have helped us along the journey."

As they talked about it, they knew they had to have food and clothing. Here it was. They felt like they were Albanian thieves themselves. Bogdon reminded them the old ones would want the boys to use them The old ones were giving the boys a chance to live, so they all agreed they could take these gifts. One boy remembered the prayer for the dead and repeated it solemnly. With difficulty, they pulled off the shoes and boots of the dead ones and loaded their knapsacks with as much food as they could carry.

Last, they covered up the bodies with branches and put rocks on top to discourage the wolves. Sadly the boys said goodbye to each grandpa and grandma. It was bitter cold now and beginning to snow again. Finally, the boys were all alone. The little band of boys, now about 30 in number, started up the mountainside following the narrow path.

By holding onto low branches, the boys pulled themselves up the first steep mountain. Sometimes they met Albanians who started to rob them. However, seeing they were boys and had nothing except the clothes they wore and their ragged knapsacks, the thieves left the boys, cursing in disappointment. Several nights some caring Albanians took them to small hunting cottages where they could sleep inside. The boys felt relief at their kindness.

Many Boys Perished from the Conditions

On other nights the boys had to lay their blankets on the snowy rocks. Almost nightly the cold and exhaustion caused another boy to give up. The remaining boys buried the bodies in the rock crevices, wrote down their names and information, and said their usual prayers.

Meanwhile, the bandits chased and robbed some of the peasants of their horses and oxen and seized their goods. Sometimes they killed or wounded the peasants, taking revenge for the recent war with Serbia. But the other Albanians did not harm the boys.

It took eight days for the boys to cross the mountains into Albania. On the way several more boys perished by freezing. Sometimes they slipped on the icy paths and almost slid down the mountainside. One boy fell and broke his arm. Stefan and Petar took some big sticks and wrapped his arm with a scarf. The boy tried hard not to cry from pain.

The older boys made a rope out of ragged shirts for each boy to hold on. The bigger boys placed themselves between the smaller ones and helped them to keep their footing at the treacherous narrow places on the path. They came upon some peasants and watched as a horse and an ox plunged down the mountainside. But the boys were too cold, exhausted and hungry to be horrified over the loss. They would face the pain and anger of those feelings in later days and months.

As they neared the end of the mountain path, some of the boys started feeling feverish and coughed frequently. They put snow on their faces to cool the fever. But the leaders realized the urgency to reach safety before the boys were too sick to continue. Nevertheless, several more boys slumped over on the path, refusing to get up. Even Branko seemed so exhausted and feverish that Stefan feared for his friend's life.

When the path finally widened, they could see the town of Scutari in the distance. This was their destination! Excitedly, Stefan and another boy half carried Branko to the path's end. They sat there and rested, then walked the last steps to Scutari. There they found food and shelter and the kind English nurses and doctors.

They had found safety. Their terrible ordeal of walking for nearly four months had finally ended, and they had miraculously survived.

These stories of the boys and of the old man and his wife are derived from oral and written accounts. The boy's names are fictitious. Of the 20,000 boys who had started the march, only about 5,000 reached the Adriatic. They were taken to the island of Vido, where they found help. More died of a typhus outbreak and were buried in the sea, a large rock tied to them so the bodies would sink. Over 5,000 soldiers also died and were buried this way.

Some of the older boys joined the army, and some younger ones went to the island of Corfu where they found homes. It is not known how many of the boys were reunited with their families. Some fortunate boys were taken to France and England where homes and schooling were provided for them. One such school was Heriot School in Edinburgh, Scotland. (see story page 104)

Some of the sick soldiers were taken to Algeria, others to Greece to recuperate or to die. The peasants also went with the soldiers. Their numbers and fate are unknown. Some of the fleeing peasants and villagers before reaching Albania had decided to go back to their homes and farms to live under the command of their enemy. As a result, thousands lost their lives to starvation, disease, cruel treatment, and even execution.

The remainder of the once proud 300,000 Serbian army was now reduced to about 150,000. But the soldiers who recovered went on to fight the Bulgarians in Greece beside the British and French.

The Serbian people lost up to 20% of their entire population, or 775,000 total deaths. Historian John Keegan says of the Serbs: "Among all the combatant nations of the war, the Serbs stood out as the supreme warrior race, tough, wily and apparently undefatigable." (From An Illustrated History of the First World War*)*

THE OLD MAN AND HIS WIFE
A Story as Envisioned by the Author

Vujadin and his wife, Milena, trudged with difficulty through the tracks left in the snow by the other peasants walking ahead of them. Slower and slower were the old couple's footsteps. They came to a rock overhang. Underneath someone had laid an old tree trunk to serve as a seat. Wearily, the man and his wife left the tracks. In mounds of snow up to their knees, they shuffled slowly to the tree trunk. Exhausted, they sat down. Neither one moved, nor paid attention to the few stragglers who called to them.

"You can't sit there and rest, Vujadin. You'll freeze to death," a friend called. Another traveler shouted, "Come on with us, old man and old woman, you can make it." Others said, "We have to keep moving, surely Albania is getting close."

The old couple ignored the calls. Their breathing became more sluggish. Milena removed the scarf that covered her long gray hair rolled in a bun. She took off her heavy wool lined leather mittens and cast them aside. Vujadin frowned, what was she doing? She would freeze. She was inviting death. He tried to cover her hair again with the scarf, but she brushed it aside. "Mother, what are you doing? I will help you to walk, we'll just rest a few minutes."

She looked at him in resignation. Her head sank onto her chest. She closed her eyes and laid her bare hands on her old woolen coat. Vujadin knew then what she was doing.

Old Man and Wife – *Drawing by Vivian Kallmann.*

He felt powerless to help her, for he was powerless to help himself. He would stay with her as long as she needed him.

Soon his breath was measured. His head hung down on the collar of his coat. He pulled off his mittens and loosened the scarf around his neck. He removed his fur cap, laying it on the tree trunk. He soon became drowsy. His hands lost all feeling as numbness sank in. His wife was motionless beside him. He breathed one more short breath. His heart beat one more time. Then nothing.

The snow began again, covering their dark coats with splotches of white.

"THE SKELETON FROM VIDO"

Interview with Daca Popovic Nadezda and Verka Popovic, daughters of the man called "Skeleton from Vido", Branko Bosilkov, interpreter and guide.

In a small cemetery near the village of Barzilevci, a stranger in a black coat and hat climbed the hill. His head appeared between tombstones as he walked down each row. He stopped in front of a large black marble monument. Standing there reverently, he removed his hat, crossed himself three times, and kissed the engraved photograph on the shiny black structure. He looked longingly at the portrait. It was of Cedo Popovic, an important Serbian hero.

The visitor said the hero's name aloud and added, "May you rest in peace." Satisfied, he replaced his black hat of European style, and looked closely at the dates on the monument: 1896-1991. Embellishing the monument were other phrases, including "Man from Salonika." On the reverse side of the structure was a small engraved photo of an exhausted Serbian soldier from World War I. An inscription reads: "Skeleton From Vido." The man knew that resting here were the bones of the man who, at the age of 19, crossed the Albanian mountains in an extremely cold wintry forced march to escape the armies of Germany, Austria-Hungary and Bulgaria.

The young man was taken by an Allied ship to Vido Island, near Corfu Island in the Adriatic Sea, where in several months he regained his health. He had dreaded being taken to Vido, because that was where the hospitals were for men not expected to survive. Vido was called "The Blue Cemetery" because the dead bodies were cast into the sea due to lack of burial space. But Cedo determined he would live. One day he was in line waiting for the French doctor to examine a row of men. The doctor would decide which would live and which ones probably would not make it. Cedo threw out his bony chest, stood straight and huffed and puffed. He said he suffered from dysentery but otherwise was not ill.

He told the doctor, "I am healthier than those others." The doctor weighed him. The scales showed 23 kilos or 73 pounds. The doctor asked if he could take Cedo's photograph, and he agreed. Several days later, Cedo learned why the photograph was taken. It had been printed worldwide. Cedo kept the photo hidden in his wallet from others.

"I kept this as my most valuable possession and did not show it to anyone. I thought a man should hide his misery from the sight of others. It should be my secret. I looked at it only one more time, and that was just before our last battle in Salonika. I told myself I survived both the Albanian Retreat and Vido Island. I will survive every other difficulty in my life."

Cedo Popovic's daughters, Daca Popovic Nadezda and Varka Popovic, hold the photo of their father taken by the French doctor. This made Cedo known to the world. *Photo by Nancy Cramer.*

About six months later, trained by French troops, he joined about 100,000 Serbs who sailed to Salonika, Greece. There for two more years Cedo and other Serbs fought the severest of battles against the Bulgarians. With Serbia in the lead, the Allies forced the Bulgarians to surrender in October 1918. The armistice was signed November 11, 1918, and he and hundreds of other Serbian soldiers began the long journey walking to their homes in Serbia. Not all the veterans had homes to return to. The Bulgarians had been vicious in burning village after village and desecrating the small churches and cemeteries.

Many years later Cedo was interviewed, and the famous photograph of him in the last stages of starvation was again published. He was dressed in ragged clothes, wearing a tall hat with a bag hanging from his left arm. He wore shoes that were falling apart. His face was pale, eyes sunken, reflecting his suffering.

His two daughters met my guide and me at the compound where their family lived. They told more stories about their famous parent. One story was when he found out the doctor had published Cedo's photograph of his starved body in worldwide newspapers. A French doctor took pity on him and brought him some precious oranges to eat. The doctor, whose name Cedo could not remember, visited him often, bringing special food. Cedo regretted he could not remember the kind doctor's name.

The photograph he always kept hidden in his wallet. The daughters repeated what their father had said about it. "I kept this as my most valuable possession and did not show to anyone. I was afraid no woman would want to marry me," he had added.

After the war he studied in Belgrade, then moved to the village near Loznica. He lived later in a humble house in the village of Brasina and married a woman named Jelka, "who saw the goodness in him," his daughters said. The couple had three daughters before Jelka died. Cedo remarried and had three more daughters. Two of them from the second marriage now live in one of the three houses in the compound. The roof leaks but they have no money to fix it. One house is maintained for the chickens running around the yard, and the other is for storage of corn and old furniture. Their father built all three of the houses.

Daca related a story her father had told about how he got the nickname "kacamak" meaning "polenta." It happened on Christmas Day 1916. He was standing in line for a bowl of warm polenta the French were feeding the Serbians. The order was for one bowl of polenta for each soldier. Cedo got his bowl and ate it quickly, he was so hungry. He managed to get back into line by hiding behind some other soldiers and got a second bowl. He gobbled it down. Once again he lined up when the officer wasn't looking and was served a third bowl. He also ate this quickly. This time the officer saw him and slapped him on the face. Cedo fell down, and the polenta came up from his stomach. Not discouraged, he scooped up what he could from the ground and ate that. This was when the other soldiers gave him the nickname.

Both daughters laughed heartily at the story. They ended their father's story by telling how he had a job as a secretary and administrator in a small town 18 kilometers away. He walked to the job and home every day. "He was a good man and a caring neighbor."

When he died in 1991, he had a military funeral and people came from all around, even some high ranking military people. Daca had three daughters who lived away, and she just recently lost her only son. Both women seemed to have inherited some of the courage their father had and are determined, like their father, to endure any hardships that might come their way.

A SERBIAN RED CROSS NURSE'S STORY
"Hell in Our Tent"—Anonymous True Story

(Unfortunately the woman's name was lost in my notes, but I am using it to illustrate that nurses also were subject to stress from their work and often became so ill they had to be repatriated. A few unfortunate nurses who had "given their all" working with the wounded, took their lives in despair, even as they were boarding ships that would take them home to England. These women need to be honored as much as the soldier on the front line.)

The nurse, in a document, begins her story: "As a young woman, I was lucky to be accepted as a nurse because the other nurses were men. I proudly put the Red Cross armband on my left arm. This was an official sign that I was now a nurse for the Serbian army. I remembered my last goodbye to my father, Arangel (spelling unknown). How proud he would be.

"In Corfu that year of 1915 the medical team had to live under a wooden shelter, as there were not enough buildings even for all the sick men. The French provided us with this place because during the crossing over the Albanian mountains, the Serbian medical teams had provided valuable aid to the sick. This shelter has dried piles of hay or chaff for us to lie on. Our Serbian staff consisted of three doctors and ten nurses. When I arrived, there were already 47 patients to be treated. Then new ones rapidly arrived, soldiers and civilians, exhausted and starving. Many were sick with dysentery and typhus.

"Patients continued to arrive for many days and nights, many only to die. The typhus hardly spared killing anyone, because the men were weak from lack of food and fatigue. When they arrived, the disease was already in its final phase. I served on night duty, and almost every half hour I had to wake up doctors to help us nurses. There were so many patients to tend to, burning with high fever and constantly moaning for water, that we often were overwhelmed.

A Red Cross unit has arrived in Salonika in late 1916. The C.M.O. and Miss Bedford are at the entrance to Ostrovo Camp. Assistant matron Harvey and her assistant Miss Reid (left) are talking to Serbians. *(Courtesy Edward Percy Stebbling from his book, "At the Serbian Front," 1917. Also Public Domain.)*

"There were also numerous people with frostbitten legs. We sent them to the French and English hospitals where the gangrenous limbs were amputated. Once I was in a tent with a little girl about five years old, who told me, 'Sister, tonight I dreamed I was dancing at some festival.' I raised the blanket that covered her and saw the right leg was blue. I knew what had happened. That day she was sent to the hospital."

"I remained on Corfu for four months. I did every job that was needed. The patients constantly showed their gratitude and always wanted me near them. It's a real miracle that they survived, considering their fragile health when they came here. Perhaps they liked me because I was young, and I would listen to the problems the young men told me. Despite the tremendous problems war posed, for the sick patient, his problems are of the first concern for him.

"About May 5, 1916, I was transferred to Salonika, Greece, by truck, then ambulance to the front lines held by the Serbian Sumadija Division. The hospital there was a huge tent with several slightly wounded soldiers inside. A doctor, some nurses and additional staff were in a dozen smaller tents surrounding the big one. I was sleeping in one of the small tents when the car came, bringing some of the English doctors to see how we, as a Serbian Red Cross group, were faring and what we needed.

Important Battle of Kajmakcalan

"We learned that the Serbian soldiers had started another difficult offensive, that of scaling the Kajmakcalan mountain near Bijola. The fighting was constant, day and night, for three months without any lapse. The wounded were brought in, 100 at a time, then 200 and 300. We treated the wounds of each and could not even close our eyes to rest. One soldier came with a big Bulgarian knife still sticking in his chest. He proudly explained that he shot the Bulgarian dead with one bullet.

"Soldiers who arrived with missing hands, arms, legs or an eye shot out, needed immediate help at the English hospitals in Salonika. Sadly, many died in the ambulances before they reached the hospitals. The hilly roads were narrow, filled with holes, and the bounce of the hard rubber tires caused many deaths from shock among these critically wounded soldiers. They did not live to see the sun set that day.

"Each patient had his own need. 'Turn me on my side.' 'I want some water.' 'I am in pain.' If there is a hell on earth, it was in our tent. White sheets quickly turned bloody red soon after a soldier was placed on the bed. Some wounded asked for water but died before I could return with the water. All were in pain. One had leg wounds when a grenade blew his feet off, but he was strangely quiet.

"Malaria came again. The fever was deadly. At the beginning of 1917 I caught the disease and then pneumonia afterwards. My sister nurses respected my work and needed me there, but they knew I must go to the Salonika hospital soon and get well. I knew they were right. I could not do my job anymore.

ENGLISH NURSE SISTER TATHAM
WRITES OF THE RETREAT

One of the nurses with Mrs. Stobart's units, **Miss M.I. Tatham**, recorded many of the trials she and other women endured in the long arduous Serbian army Retreat of winter 1915. She wrote about the mud clinging to the women's skirts until they finally pinned up the skirts to what was considered a decent measure. One's ankles were decently covered encased in high leather boots. This was one of the few problems that had an easy solution. The Serbians named the mud, "the little friend of Serbia," because it also delayed the advance of enemy soldiers. The story of Serbian Volunteer Division Retreat is told with the usual "Keep Calm and Carry On" motto typical of many English people.

Miss Tatham's story of the Retreat began with the evacuation of Mrs. Stobart's hospital at Kragauyevatz. Moving such a large field hospital under wartime conditions required coordination, calmness of nerve, many strong arms, and many more bullocks to pull the huge number of carts readily available. However, the persevering English medical team, along with their Serbian helpers and some Austrian prisoners of war, were equal to the task.

The dismaying news was that the only railroad line from Belgrade to Salonika in Greece had been cut the day before by the Bulgarians. Telephone wires also had been severed, meaning communication with the outside world was nonexistent. This was a problem that often perplexed the Serbians. Not deterred, Miss Tatham arranged for the needed bullocks and carts to pull the precious hospital equipment and supplies. A car was procured to transport her team, but it often broke down or became stuck in deep mud holes. Despite this delay of the peasants' retreat, they extended the best possible hospitality to the English under the circumstances.

Soldier father weeps at grave of his dead soldier son. *Public Domain***.*

This caused Mrs. Stobart to remark, "Here, as always in Serbia, we were reminded of the dominance of war as a factor in the lives of the people." One old woman who had come for medical aid asked another old woman, "In which war was I born?" "It was the 1848 war with Austria," was her answer.

The long line of refugees was stopped constantly by a cart that turned over; an ox or horse that dropped in the path either because of exhaustion or death; the artillery guns coming past them with soldiers shouting loudly, "Move over, out of our way!" or officials in their automobiles honking at stray pigs or sheep who escaped the crook of their peasant owner. The medical teams treated wounded soldiers who came to them and cared for sick civilians as well. Sometimes they set up their tents to take care of the mass of retreating soldiers which included the "*cheechas*" or "uncles," as the old veterans were called. The "*cheechas*" defended the rear of the line, allowing the younger men to retreat. Theirs was a dangerous job, and they bore the brunt of the casualties, being closest to the enemy.

Loud, noisy, the road was cluttered with people, vehicles, carts, and guns. Miss Tatham longed for the night's rest to come sooner. Sometimes they stopped early, if rooms could be obtained by the guide at the next inn. Several times they lodged in the huge courtyards of local monasteries enclosed by thick mud brick walls. This meant a dinner of hot soup, for the monks kept their fires burning night and day for use by uninvited exhausted guests.

Despite the unusual December cold weather, a dip in the icy stream meant a refreshing wash. When staying several nights at an inn or monastery, the travelers washed their clothes, hanging them in the icy air to dry.

The Serbians demonstrated "high courage" as they struggled with the conditions. Miss Tatham passed by men who lay dead by the side of the road, waiting for "the snow to shroud their body."

Icy Path Fatal to People and Animals

In the higher passes of the 8,000 feet high mountains, the left side was a sheer drop to the river 1,000 feet below. The narrow path, slippery with ice or deep in snow, was not wide enough to allow two mules to pass each other. Some animals and people slipped on the ice and plunged to the roaring river below to drown or freeze to death. There was no help to give them. On several of the coldest nights, the mules, if left outside the tent or room, froze to death. Their blankets and gear were then packed, if possible, on another shivering, starving little animal.

At night, the refugees and soldiers set up tents, making fires and singing or dancing the "kola," if the Germans were far enough behind for safety. One time the medical teams camped in an old 13th century monastery, far back in the mountains. They rested for two weeks, before they received the order to move on. Their next stop was Rashka, where hot cocoa and soup cheered their bodies and spirits. However, Miss Tatham primly wrote that their sleeping quarters were one large room crammed with

Serbian soldier holds his head in despair. *Public Domain****.

smelly unwashed bodies. The soldiers' uniforms were in tatters. No new uniforms were available as the making of shells had taken precedence over the manufacture of uniforms. Most of the soldiers still had not recovered from the wars of 1912 and 1913, and many wore uniforms from that service.

Miss Tatham, when asked where was the support from England and France, politely reminded the Serbs that all of Europe was engaged in the conflict, including England "in her own bitter struggle."

The Plight of the Serbian People on the Retreat

The most disappointing day for many refugees occurred when they were only two days from their goal of Monastir in southern Serbia, near the Greek border. The news came that the Bulgarians had already occupied the city. The refugees had no choice but to turn back and head north-west for the mountains of Montenegro and Albania. They had hoped to avoid crossing those dangerous mountains, but as Miss Tatham wrote, with grit and luck, many of them made the hazardous passage.

On the day they eventually reached the port of departure in Albania, the skies cleared, the gray clouds disappeared, and the eternal rain ceased. The ships lay waiting for them, the ones that had survived the torpedoes of the Austrian navy the day before. Their sunken funnels protruded out of the water, and all the precious foodstuffs wasted away in the sea. But the promise had been kept for Miss Tatham and those who arrived with her. They would be taken to a port of safety, leaving the horrors of the war behind them.

DEPARTURE FROM MOTHER SERBIA
A Story as Envisioned by the Author

We saw the ships in the harbor as we stumbled down the last of the mountain paths. Five Italian ships were waiting near the shore for us to board. Exhausted beyond belief, we doubted if we would have the strength to board the ships. And where was this safe place the ships were taking us to? Our doubts vanished when a French officer, followed by men carrying stretchers, approached our leader. Soon, those of us able to walk, started toward the dock, some supported by French soldiers, some limping by themselves.

Others were loaded onto stretchers, and the bearers headed toward a different dock. The stretchers were laid carefully in small boats, and sailors rowed them to a ship. When fully loaded, two of those ships headed to the island of Corfu. Sailors on the deck and the upper lines were assigned to watch for German mines and submarine trails. None of us were out of danger yet. The Italians and French sailors, in rescuing us Serbians, had placed themselves in the same danger.

The process of loading almost 7,000 Serbian soldiers into the last three ships, lasted long past dark. Lanterns lit the beaches until the last dock was cleared of all of us. The shadows of the lanterns cast eerie scenes in the darkness making weird sights. Earlier in the daylight, the scenes had also borne a sense of unreality. The English medical teams gathered their equipment and went back to their nearby headquarters, waiting for a group of soldiers to make the final descent to the beach. These also were wounded men in filthy bandages, sick men in soiled uniforms, faces unshaved for months, and hands unwashed for days. Spectors of men. Starving. Shrunken as they were, how could they still be alive? Some were to die on the trip. Others would last days, even weeks. Still others would recover their health miraculously and head for Greece where at the Bulgarian and Serbian borders, they would fight and defeat the Bulgarians. (continued on page 88)

This type of German submarine patrolled the Adriatic Sea and torpedoed some of the Allied ships rescuing the Serbs waiting on the shores. *Public Domain.*

Leaving Serbia in a small boat bound for the ship which will carry this soldier and thousands of others to safety in Corfu and other sites. *Drawing by Vivian Kallmann.*

Reaching The Island of Corfu

Once the first ship began its 24-hour trip to Vido Island, near Corfu, some of us received care and feeding by the English medics on board. Some of us were fed broth or even just water. No one's needs were met fully. There were too many of us. We had too many needs. Most slept restlessly with a blanket covering us from the night's chilly air. A fortunate few had bunks with straw mattresses. Caretakers of the men rarely left the side of their assigned Serbians, distasteful and odorous as those wounded might be.

Near dawn the ship's engines roared to a stop. "Nous avon ici! (We are here)" was the cry I heard. The Serbs lying on the deck raised their heads at the cry. They saw land covered with trees. On a long beach many soldiers, nurses, doctors, ox carts and wagons pulled by mules were waiting. "Have we reached Corfu?" asked one Serb of a Frenchman, who shook his head, not understanding his question. "Yes," said another Frenchman, guessing at the meaning. "C'est le terre. (It is land.)"

The first ship dropped anchor. The second one arrived several hours later. The Serbians left the ship in a similar manner as they had been loaded. The sick and wounded on stretchers were carefully laid onto horse drawn wagons, accompanied by medical personnel. Others were laid on the beds of trucks and wagons and taken to a different place. Special carts were brought for those who could sit up and ride.

No one had to walk anymore. At least not for now. I had worn out three pair of *opanki,* then found some leather boots on a dead soldier that fit. He had no more use for them. When they wore out, I bound my feet with strips of cloth torn from blankets of those who no longer needed them either. The strips were in shreds when I reached the beach.

I looked behind at the sea as the wagons began moving. There, miles away lay my homeland, my family and my previous life. I was leaving behind the glorious 800-year-old history of our Serbia. I was leaving behind nearly four months of fighting and retreating, never knowing if I would live or die. Behind were the freezing days and icy nights, shortage of clothing, lack of ammunition, never enough food. Then climbing, ever climbing, the more than 7,000 feet of the Albanian mountains.

Behind lay the dead. We had no time to bury them. Brothers, cousins, comrades. Some injured so badly they would die soon, all alone. I remembered when we passed burned out villages, villages that we had fought over, attacked, recaptured, then finally abandoned. Somehow, even I, a farmer, could barely endure the stench of dead oxen and horses. I passed our sacred churches with only walls remaining, the interior hollowed out by constant enemy shelling. I marched with eyes filling with tears near desecrated cemeteries, where for hundreds of years our namesakes had been buried.

Some soldiers asked themselves, "We left all this behind, and for what future?" I had no answer for them. Other survivors voiced their doubts. "Better to be dead back in Serbia than homeless, sick, with no heart left to grieve." I wondered, "Who can endure such loss? With no heart left within him to grieve? Were the desperate efforts to stay alive worth the struggle, when I can't feel sadness or grief?"

Why Have Our Lives Been Spared?

Some soldiers I was sure felt gratitude for their rescue and for the care they were to receive. But others questioned why their lives had been preserved. Why Bojan or Dragan had been shot or frozen to death. Why the lives of their uncle and father were spared as victims to the war, when the youngest sons died.

"Did God's hand reach down and touch the wrong one to die?" I asked my patron saint. "Perhaps the priest could explain God's choices. Or if he could not, who can? As for me, I don't want to live without knowing these answers. Without any answers, I can not face my mother and receive her sorrow or her anger."

The Soldier saw other Serbs lying on stretchers perhaps with no thoughts. Just exhaustion. They wanted release, release that wore the face of death. Others wanted nothing. Nothing at all.

POSTSCRIPT:

At last, in 1918, after nearly six hundred years as a country under the rule of the Ottoman Empire, it officially became "The Republic of Serbia, the Croats and Slovenes" by the terms of the Treaty of Versailles signed in Paris in June 1919. Once again Serbia ruled her own people.

Serbia's
Coat of Arms

Prince Regent Aleksander, son of King Petar, who took over the command in 1915 because of his father's failing eyesight. The Prince traveled every mile of kilometer of the march along with his troops. He became official ruler of Serbia in 1921 when his father died. He ruled until he was assassinated in 1934 in France while on an official visit. The assassin was Bulgarian, a member of a Macedonian revolutionary group. The king was 43 years old when he died. *Public Domain.*

King Petar Karadjordevic, who took over as ruler of Serbia on June 2, 1903. He was the first constitutional monarch elected by parliament. He enacted legislation to reform the constitution, the army and educational systems and distribution of land. He went on the Retreat with his Army, at times walking, riding his horse, or driving an oxen cart. He reentered Belgrade in triumph on November 3, 1918 after the Bulgarians surrendered earlier to the Serbs. He was much revered by his people. *Public Domain.*

PART EIGHT

SAFETY AWAITS AT CORFU

CORFU—ISLAND OF LIFE AND ISLAND OF DEATH
A Story as Envisioned by the Author

Supporting themselves with their rifles, hundreds of the sick and wounded Serbian soldiers made their way up the beach of Corfu to where the wagons waited. Some French soldiers, seeing how helpless some of the Serbs were, rushed down to help them. On another part of the beach, stretcher bearers were carrying the sickest cases to special wagons where the stretchers were being loaded. All was done with precision and without haste, as if this procedure had been practiced many times before.

The Soldier stood by one wagon and saw a face he recognized. "Hallo, Zeliko! So you made it across the mountain;" he thought and was grateful his friend was still alive. The man groaned and moved, revealing a large bandage-covered wound across his abdomen. "He won't last long," The Soldier thought sadly. "Those are among the worst wounds. Head wounds are usually fatal too." His thoughts were interrupted as the wagon driver cracked his whip and the slow sturdy oxen began to haul the load down the path toward the tent hospital.

Serbian soldiers would erect a marker or cross in one of the many places where lives were lost, or important events took place. The simple, even primitive marker became special and heartwarming. *Public Domain****.

The Soldier walked over to the next wagon. It was loaded with boys of all ages. Some were crying for their mothers, others were moaning with pain, while some sat silently, numb with disbelief. One of the English nurses moved around the boys, carefully in the crowded wagon, patting a head here and there, giving a smile that was weakly returned. She gave water to one boy but shook her head when he asked for bread. They were too weak to eat solid food now. Broth would be given to them soon. The Soldier thought it was miraculous that any of the boys had survived the rigorous conditions of the march. Of course, many had not. He had passed by bodies lying three or four to a heap, as if they were still trying to warm themselves by huddling together. He shook his head at the memory.

The loading of the ox carts and wagons continued past dark. Flaming torches had been set up on the beach, making shadows of the figures working to transfer all the remaining Serbs to their conveyances. The scene was ghastly and eerie, just as it had been on the beaches of the Adriatic when the refugees were loaded into the waiting rescue ships. All was spectral and shadowy. All was unreal. It would take days of rest, a clean bed and clothes, and food, especially food, to begin to erase the grimness of the Retreat.

The Retreat had begun December 10, 1915, when the Serbian First Army withdrew as the rearguard in Mojkovac near the border of Herzogovina. The Montenegrins were left by themselves to combat the better equipped and armed Austrian army. The Austrian army was three times or more the size of the defenders. Andrej Mitrovic in his book, *Serbia's Great War 1914-1918*, writes that the Montenegrin army was "to fight its most glorious battles of the World War." Their defense helped ensure the safety of the Serbian army, still waiting vainly to be rescued on the Adriatic coast. Then the ships stopped coming and bewilderment set in. Finally, the Allies appeared and rescued the Serbian government officials, taking them to Brindisi, Italy, and on to Corfu. Ultimately, the Montenegrins, greatly outmanned by the Austrian-Hungarians, signed a treaty of capitulation. King Nicolas left the country for exile without leaving any directions for the country's future after the war.

After a month, only one-tenth of the refugees had been removed to safety, so the remaining 140,000 had to march farther south down the coast to Durres and Vlore to escape the Austrian planes that fired on the refugees on the beaches. German submarines had torpedoed ships on their way to the harbor. This extra walking meant up to about 120 more miles through hazardous terrain.

More Allied Ships Helped with the Rescue

Then the English, French, and Italian ships began to make more frequent trips, despite the danger of German submarines, which at one time torpedoed five Allied ships in the harbor. By February 15, 1916, about 90,000 soldiers and 5,000 civilians had been rescued. A few days later Prince Aleksander and his command were taken to Corfu with 120,000 other Serbs. He had stayed behind with his people. More than 135,000 people were rescued later, followed by another 10,000. Yet there were still some Serbian units that remained in Albania, waiting for transportation. The last soldiers to leave were the cavalry division which boarded ships as late as April 5, 1916.

Though the Allies were often criticized for getting a late start in setting up the evacuation plan, it must be remembered that German submarines were active in the Atlantic waters and were aware of the rescue plan. Also England had to use her ships to bring supplies from India and Australia for the fighting on the Western Front, so the whole rescue was a remarkable effort by the Allies. This was another time that England's fleet, the largest in the world, was invaluable to the war effort. Nevertheless, King Petar was quoted as saying, "Even if Serbia survives, I fear there soon will be no Serbs."

And there was some truth to his words when those in Corfu began to die from disease and other causes. Nearly 5,000 soldiers died in the first two months on Corfu. On the island of Vido, where the sickest had been taken, the death count was about 5,400. Because the small island could accommodate only so many bodies, every day small boats were loaded with the dead. Their bodies had rocks tied around them and they were taken out to the bay. There the corpses were dropped overboard. The blue sea waters became their shroud and their grave. The Serbs have two poignant songs, "The Blue Sea" and "There, Far Away," which honor these dead.

"Plava Grobnica" or The Blue Graveyard

Gazite tihim hodom!
Opelo gordo držim u doba jeze noćne
Nad ovom svetom vodom.

Tu na dnu, gde školjke san umoran hvata
I na mrtve alge tresetnica pada,
Leži groblje hrabrih, leži brat do brata,
Prometeji nade, apostoli jada.

Zar ne osećate kako more mili,
Da ne ruši večni pokoj palih četa?
Iz dubokog jaza mirni dremež čili,
A umornim letom zrak meseca šeta.

To je hram tajanstva i grobnica tužna
Za ogromnog mrca, k'o naš um beskrajna.
Tiha kao ponoć vrh ostrvlja južna,
Mračna kao savest, hladna i očajna.

Zar ne osećate iz modrih dubina
Da pobožnost raste vrh voda prosuta
I vazduhom igra čudna pitomina?
To velika duša pokojnika luta

Stojte, galije carske! Na grobu braće moje
Zavite crnim trube.
Stražari u svečanom opelo nek otpoje
Tu, gde se vali ljube!

Jer proći će mnoga stoleća, k'o pena
Što prolazi morem i umre bez znaka,
I doći će nova i velika smena,
Da dom sjaja stvara na gomili

Walk with silent tread
I am officiating a proud Requiem in the chill of the night
Upon these sacred waters.

There at the bottom, where seashells fall into the tired grip of sleep
And peat falls upon the dead algae,
Lay graves of the brave, lay brother to brother
Prometheus's of Hope, Apostles of Pain.

Do you not feel how the sea calms,
That it may not trouble the fallen troop's eternal rest?
From the deep abyss peaceful slumber ebbs,
And tired flight of the moonbeam walks.

This is a temple of secret, and a graveyard of sorrow
For the great dead, endless as our mind.
Silent as midnight upon southern islands,
Dark as a conscience, cold and despairing.

Do you not feel from azure depths,
That piety grows spilled atop these waters
And the air is filled with curious gentleness?
It is the great soul of the fallen, roaming.

Halt, imperial galleys! Before the tomb of my brothers
Shroud your trumpets in black.
Let your liveried sentries chant the holy dirge
Here, where waves embrace!

For the centuries will pass, like white foam
That crosses the sea and dies without trace,
And a new and great age will come,
And make a splendid home upon a pile of graves.

But this graveyard, where lays buried
The terrible, secret epic,
Will cradle a fairytale for the ages
Where the spirit will seek out its coryphaeus's.

Buried are here garlands of days past
And the fleeting joy of an entire nation,
And so this cemetery lies in the shadow of the waves
Between the bosom of the earth and the celestial vault.

Halt, imperial galleys! Extinguish your torches,
And draw your oars to rest,

Serbian version on the left and English version on right. *Public Domain.*

French medical personnel reported seeing dead bodies piled up like "planks of wood on top of each other, four in a row, sometimes six…" On Vido, named the "island of death," more than 5,400 Serbs died, and 1,000 died in Bizerta, Italy, where more sick soldiers had taken refuge. Most deaths were due to the spread of diseases.

Gradually the weather improved, and enough tents had arrived for shelter. The Serbs began to get well. Soon the Serbs set up army style camps and began physical training in preparation for instruction on how to use the new weapons the French were to supply. Their physical health and rising spirit drew admiration from other Army officers. The recovery was deemed "miraculous."

The Army had left Corfu for Salonika by the end of 1916, but the government stayed on in exile until October 6, 1918. In the postwar treaties, the land of Serbia was to be combined with other lands and called "The Kingdom of the Serbs, Croats, and Slovenes" with a constitutional monarch under Prince Aleksander of the Karadjordevic dynasty. The name of the kingdom was changed to Yugoslavia in 1929. But the country had a troubled existence, partly because of tensions between the dominant Serbs and the nationalist Croatians. The Serbs' suffering did not end with the conclusion of World War I. During the Nazi occupation in World War II even more atrocities and misery came to the courageous Serbians.

There, Far Away

There, far away,
Far away from the sea,
There is my homeland,
There is my Serbia.

There, far away,
Where the yellow lemons blooms
There was to the Serbian Army,
The only open way.

There, far away
Where the white lily blooms,
There their lives laid down
Father and son together.

Without my motherland,
I lived on Corfu,
But I always cheered,
"Long live my Serbia!"

The English physician, **Dr. Isabelle Hutton**, recorded in her notes: "As soon as a Serbian person recovers, he starts to sing and dance. This was in his character and an integral part of life; just as tilling the land. Their favorite song was "There, Far Away." The song is about leaving one's home and country and it expresses the longing for home. Some of us women sang together with the soldiers, and through the song's many verses, we got to like that beautiful language."

The nurse-soldier-hero woman **Milunka Savic**, whom the French compared to as the Serbian Joan of Arc, is quoted as saying: "We used to sing when it was most difficult for us. We sang when the French ships transported us from Albania to… Corfu, when we were just skin and bones. The French sailors and officers cried when they heard us singing and they said: 'What a formidable nation!' We sang when we were dying on the island of Vido, and we sang when we were dying on the Thessaloniki Front." (It was reportedly written by Dorde Marinkovic on Corfu in 1916 and has many versions.)

OTHER IMPORTANT SERBIAN WOMEN IN THE WAR—

Nedezda Petrovic- gave up her artist reputation as one of Servia's most significant women painters of her time to become a nurse. She served in both Balkan Wars in the years 1912-1913 before she died of typhus during the epidemic in Valijevelo in 1915. A monument was built in her honor in 1955 and a museum 20 years later. *Courtesy of PanaComp Wonderland Travel, Serbia.*

Nadezda Petrovic
Artist Becomes Nurse

Ms. Petrovic, Serbia's most famous impressionist and fauvist, exchanged her painter's smock and brushes for the typical nurse's uniform and equipment to take the part of a volunteer in the two Balkan Wars of 1912 and 1913. In 1913, she contracted the typhus disease, which spread in epidemic proportions and also cholera. Once she became healthy enough, she resumed nursing when the Austrians attacked Serbia and the army desperately needed medical personnel.

However, it was a great loss for Serbia's art world when she later died of typhus on April 3, 1915. She was awarded a medal for bravery and the Order of the Red Cross.

Milunka Savic: A Serbian Woman Takes Role As Soldier In The Front Lines

Wanting to save her little brother from recruitment, Milunka Savic cut her long hair and donned an oversized Serbian uniform to serve in his place in battles. She began her soldiering in the Balkan Wars, then continued after the Austrian invasion. Born in a small village near Raska, she changed her first name to Milun, the masculine form of Milunka. During the fighting, she was wounded four times. It was at this last time during the second Balkan War the thing she had dreaded happened—it was discovered she was a woman. A bullet wound in her chest revealed her secret.

LEFT: Soflja Jovanovic, a lieutenant on the first day of the war, July 29, crossed the Sava River and placed a Serbian flag in front of the Austrian-Hungarian barracks. She participated in all four years of the war and was decorated with numerous Serbian medals. *Public Domain.*

RIGHT: Ljubica Cakarevic, a school teacher, volunteered in the army and on one occasion, she sneaked through Bulgarian camps in her effort to escape from Serbia and join the troops in Salonika. She was decorated with the "Milos Obilic" Gold Medal for Heroism. *Public Domain.*

When the Austrians invaded Serbia in 1914, she asked permission to fight as a woman combatant and asked Duke (Voyada) Putnik himself for a rifle. Against his advice for her to serve as a nurse, she insisted upon having a rifle. At war's end she was honored as a member of the second most elite infantry regiment, the "Iron Regiment."

When the fighting ceased, she received twelve Serbian and Allied medals for bravery and became one of the most decorated soldiers in the Serbian army. Her battle feats became legendary.

"THE STRICKEN LAND, SERBIA"
As Seen Through the Eyes of Dr. C. Leake Askew

One of several books available that were published in English about Serbia's retreat from the Central Powers in 1915 was written by Dr. C. Leake Askew, an English doctor, and his wife, Alice. He was attached to the First British Field for Serbia in April 1915. In his book, *The Stricken Land Serbia As We Saw It*, Dr. Askew described the terrors of the march; the death and dying of men and animals; the ever constant threat of starvation or freezing to death; and the attacks by local Arnauts (Albanians).

During the Retreat, his hospital group that was attached to the Second Serbian Army was answerable to only Serbian military authorities. Such authorities, however, made special efforts to ensure the safety of the Askews and other English staff as much as possible under the existing conditions. Sir Ralph Paget, English representative to Serbia, was assigned the responsibility for these various "missions," so the medical teams were ostensibly under the protection of the British government.

As his team took part in the Retreat, Dr. Askew wrote about seeing this scene: "The same hideous pictures—dead and dying horses…all along the road; dying soldiers continued to drop out of the ranks; a terrible depression seemed to hang…All around was the spirit of death and decay..." The "bruised and naked feet had ceased to tread the march's cruel path…in their torn and tattered uniforms…They were the martyrs of the march."

He continued with a description of "the terrors of the famous Vizier's Bridge, which has so precipitous an incline that, slippery as it was with a covering of ice, men and horses failed to negotiate it, but slid down and perished in the freezing waters below."

When his group finally scaled the mountains, after Austrian airplanes had bombed small villages where they stayed overnight and other times for several days, the group expected to find relief from the enemy. Not so. The Austrian planes flew over and attacked helpless clusters of shelterless people on the beaches of the Adriatic Sea. The author described the ports as filled with carcasses of Allied ships that had been sunk by submarines or bombs, before the ships could unload their priceless cargos of food and supplies. Some ships were bombed and sank even as they were loading their new cargo of refugees.

Albanian houses, sparsely populating the mountains, were described as forts with thick walls surrounding the houses. Only a few narrow slit windows, used as gun slots, allowed light and air into the house. It often was out of desperation to find shelter that the English team and others approached such a stronghold to seek lodgings. Sometimes they were warmly welcomed, as long as there were gold napoleon coins amongst the travelers. (Gold napoleon coins had the value of a 20 franc French gold coin. No paper money was accepted by the Albanians.)

Perhaps the most poignant part of his book is the "Epilogue: A Little Grey Cross." The cross he refers to is a simple stone monument situated on the Island of Vido, near Corfu, where the seriously ill soldiers and refugees were taken to die. Vido became "a soldier's graveyard. The living feel that they have no place on Vido…it has become a tomb—a very sacred tomb—and island of rest and sleep." A permanent sleep, the reader will understand.

The Stone Cross on Vido Island was erected in 1922 in memory of the more than 5,000 soldiers and civilians who died there after surviving the rigors and dangers of the Retreat. *Public Domain.*

The cross, engraved in both English and Serbian, was created by Serbian friends. Its lack of ostentation imitates the humbleness of the soldiers who died there. The dead bodies were taken out to the blue waters that surrounded Vido Island and cast into the sea. A soldier poet, Milutin Bojic, wrote the moving poem, *Plava Grobinica*, or *Ode to a Blue Sea Tomb*, after arriving safely in Corfu from the Retreat. Unfortunately, he died in Salonika from tuberculosis.

Final comments by Dr. Askew tell us about the upright behavior of troops recuperating on Corfu. They were law abiding; they refrained from public drunkenness and from insulting local women; and they conducted themselves without quarrelling or creating any disturbances in public. "Few armies can boast of such qualities," Dr. Clarke concluded, reflecting again his admiration for the Serbian soldier.

Such were the private thoughts and the public report of one of England's distinguished physicians who, along with his wife, endured the torments, both mental and physical, of the Retreat of the Serbian army.

THE PEASANTS TELL THEIR STORY
A Story as Envisioned by the Author

All was hustle and flurry when the word spread that the Germans were only 20 kilometers behind, at the most. The Serbian troops had already passed by the village, trailing their artillery in the mud. The mother commanded the children to listen and do exactly what she said. They had no time to waste. Jakov and Gavrilo were to yoke the oxen to the cart. "It would take the two of them," she said, "because you are young and small, but you can do it."

She turned to the girls, telling Jovanka to fold up the quilts on the big bed, and Anka to do the same on the small beds. They were to bring them to the cart and the mother would do the packing. "First," she told the old grandmother, "get your Bible and your precious things and wrap them in a kerchief. We don't want our family things to be left behind." Then she turned to the last girl waiting, who was not able to do things right although she tried. "Slavka, you get the aprons and coats for all of us. That's a good girl," she patted her on the back and turned her toward the door.

"Now, what do I need to get? We'll need cooking pots, my dried fruit and vegetables we picked. Quickly, she moved about and handed them to Slavka who had tossed the coats into the cart. "Take these to the cart. I'll arrange them later." The family consisting of a mother, grandmother, and five children, hastily packed the cart and took their place in the parade of carts already leaving the little village.

The first few weeks were uneventful. The old grandmother and the littlest girl sat in the wagon. The others walked alongside the oxen, occasionally coaxing them to pull harder. Sometimes they had to stop to allow soldiers to ride by on horses or for oxen hauling the heavy guns. Other times, someone ahead had an axle break or a wheel come off. Then everyone came to a standstill while repairs were hurriedly made. Everyone became tired, but tempers were kept under control. Fear of the Germans made them work together as they always had when fields needed more help.

At nighttime, they camped in small groups. Firewood was still available in the forested hills nearby. Everyone shared what they could, but no one was wasteful. They had been through a famine just the year before when the typhus epidemic took many lives, including the man of the family. If the man had survived, he would have gone in 1914 to fight the Austrian-Hungarians or the Germans. Once again the burdens of the household fell upon the wife. The Retreat was tiring, but they made good progress.

Then suddenly the rains came. They drenched the cover of the cart where inside sat the old grandmother and sometimes the smallest girl, Jasna, only five years old. She walked some but it was hard to keep pace even with the slow oxen. Now the rains were pouring down, making deep mud of the ruts in the primitive road. The mud tugged at their shoes, almost pulling them off, which the boys finally did. They were used to going barefoot in the summer when watching the sheep or tending the pigs.

They came to a roaring river that once was a slow flowing stream. A group of villagers discussed the hazards of crossing and finally came to a plan. The strongest oxen and cart would be led by two men, one on each side, to find their footing. They would choose what seemed to be the best place with the lowest banks. Other men would stand by to help if the cart overturned. They tried it, and although the first cart wobbled several times, it stayed upright. The few men available volunteered to take turns helping each cart across the stream. The women and older children would cling to the sides of the cart. The smaller ones would ride inside. It came time for the mother's cart to cross over. Anxiously she took off her shoes and tied up her skirts as high as was decent, and she and her sons took their places on the sides of the cart. The men coaxed the oxen to start, but the stubborn beasts looked at the water and stood firm. Finally, a small whip convinced them to step into the water. They had never felt the lash of a whip before, only a stick.

They plunged in, the cart jolted, and those inside held tightly to the ribs of the drenched cover. Slowly, with two men in front and two men in back, they guided the cart

Serbian refugees fleeing advancing enemy armies in 1915. *Public Domain.*

through the swirling waters. The men held fast to the outside ribs of the cart, occasionally almost losing their balance in the rough motion of the water. They made the crossing and the oxen started up the slippery bank. Somehow, they dug their sharp hooves into the mud. At last, with one final effort the mighty beasts reached the grassy top of the bank. A big cheer went up from the onlookers. The men, holding each other's hands and a rope tossed to them, crossed back to help the next wagon across, until finally all the villagers landed safely on the bank.

The mother ordered the oxen to be unhooked from their yoke and led over to a large patch of grass. "They need the grass like I need a cup of coffee with one, no, two, no, three spoons of sugar." But she knew she had little coffee left and the sugar supply was gone. So the oxen had the feast. Finally, after traveling several hours, the villagers decided to camp for the night. The rains had stopped, that meant fires to warm themselves after the exhausting journey. The rains would start again tomorrow. Little did they suspect that in a week, an early but heavy snowfall would begin which brought worse dangers than they had experienced up to then.

Some fortunate villagers had relatives in the high hills and sought refuge with them. Others, too tired and discouraged, turned around to return to burned out homes and damaged fields, the work of the Austrians. Some even became victims of Austrian or Bulgarian atrocities, including death by hanging. In one village, 19 peasants were tied together and set on fire. Other bodies were badly mutilated. It was if humanity had returned to its worse self.

The war cast its own curse on the peasant in ways that would equal some of the hardships their soldiers were enduring. War had no friends. It took no sides, and it spared no one of any age in its path. The Serbian peasants knew too well. Ask them.

A typical Serbian Orthodox Church from the 15th or 16th century. *Photo by Nancy Cramer.*

PART NINE

VICTORY AND THE AFTERMATH

VICTORIOUS AT LAST

Beginning on April 1, 1916, hundreds of Serbian soldiers started their journey to Salonika to fight the Bulgarians who now controlled the southern and eastern parts of Serbia. The Serbian troops, outfitted in new French uniforms but wearing the traditional *sajcaka* cap of their homeland and carrying new French-made rifles, stepped proudly down the gangplanks of the Allied ships to the port of Salonika. Theirs had not been an easy or pleasant voyage. The Greeks had refused to allow the ships to take the faster route, so the ships had to dodge the infestation of submarines stationed at the Cycladic Islands.

By the end of May, however, with no submarines attacking the convoys, 112,000 Serbians and 8,000 horses landed safely in Greece. Added to this number were some 1,700 Bosnian soldiers who had been fighting with the Montenegrins, forming a South Slav battalion as part of the French army. The Bosnians were originally part of the Austrian-Hungarian armies, but as had happened in other parts of the empire, soldiers of Slavic origins escaped when they had the opportunity to join a Serbian unit.

The victorious Serbian advance in the mountains east of Monastir: An observation post on a rocky eminence. Public Domain. Courtesy Dr. Matt Osborne.

Because of the previous Serbian wars in 1912 and 1913, many men of draft age had been killed or wounded. The men arriving now were either younger or much older in age. The British and French wondered how the new soldiers would react, even though Serbian soldiers were honored and reknown for their courage and fighting qualities.

Serbians scaled the walls of the Kajmakcalan Mountain in a feat not replicated since their forefathers, under Stephen the Mighty, fought there 550 years before. This is in Salonika in September 1916. *Public Domain.*

ABOVE: Tent hospital set up by Scottish Women's nurses in Ostrovo. Shown are the hospital wards, with the Operations Theater, in the shadow in left hand corner. The head of Lake Ostrovo is seen at the back. This hospital made of tents is typical of the ones used in the Serbian war. *Public Domain.*

LEFT: An American Red Cross Dental Station in Serbia, less than a mile from the front lines. *Public Domain.*

Le Petit Journal

ADMINISTRATION
61, RUE LAFAYETTE, 61
Les manuscrits ne sont pas rendus

On s'abonne sans frais
dans tous les bureaux de poste

5 CENT.   SUPPLÉMENT ILLUSTRÉ   5 CENT.

25ᵐᵉ Année   ✦✦   Numéro 1.275

DIMANCHE 9 AOUT 1914

ABONNEMENTS

SEINE et SEINE-ET-OISE   2 fr.   3 fr. 50
DÉPARTEMENTS   2 fr.   4 fr.
ÉTRANGER   2.50   5 fr.

LE CONFLIT ENTRE L'AUTRICHE ET LA SERBIE
La population serbe acclame les troupes

MIGRATION OF THE SERBS, A FAMOUS PAINTING BY PAJA JOVANOVIC, C. 1896, OLD SERBIA IN 1690 – 1691

DEPICTS THE SERBIANS, LED BY ARCHBISHOP ARSENIJE III, FLEEING NORTHWARD FROM THE BATTLE AT KACANIK GORGE, WHERE THE HAPSBURGS DEFEATED THE SERBS. THE SERBS WERE TRYING TO FREE THEIR COUNTRY FROM THE OTTOMAN EMPIRE AND HAD SUPPORTED A HAPSBURG INVASION INTO THE BALKANS TO HELP THEM.

KING PETAR LEADS THE RETREAT PAST BROKEN OX CARTS, FROZEN BODIES, IN THE MIDST OF DEEP SNOW AND BELOW FREEZING TEMPERATURES. COPY OF ORIGINAL PAINTING IN BELGRADE NATIONAL MUSEUM,; COPY OWNED BY LAZAR JOHANOVIC. PERMISSION TO USE GRANTED BY THE MUSEUM.

Serbian refugees, without their men, return to find remains of their homes and fields after the fighting has left the area. *Public Domain.*

A number of small battles took place, leading up to the first of the bigger campaigns. This was the capture of Monastir on Nov. 19, 1916 when General Misic commanded the Serbians, and the English Lt. Gen. George F. Milne headed the British troops. They worked well together, and it was this cooperation among these two leaders that contributed much to the successful campaigns. The French General Maurice Sarrail headed the entire Salonika campaign, and his plans differed from those of the Allied generals back in Paris, which led to some problems.

The Serbs attacked in early September and took the foothills without difficulty. A forest of beech trees hid Bulgarian machine guns, and fighting resorted to hand to hand combat with bayonets. Thereafter, bare mountainsides were exposed, each gully and trench being occupied by Bulgarians. Gradually the Serbians of the Drina Division reached the summit, capturing 50 Bulgarian prisoners. For a brief time the Serbian flag flew over a small piece of Serbian soil that had been finally re-captured.

The Bulgarians did not surrender the mountain without a counterattack

Wives also helped their husband in a few of the critical battles. If caught by the Austrians, however, retribution was swift and hard, and the women were often hanged or massacred. *Public Domain***.*

A French priest tends to the grave of a countryman in Belgrade Cemetery for French soldiers. *Public Domain****.

days later. Despite the Serbs hauling mountain guns to where Bulgarians had been positioned, the Drina Division was forced to fall back. General Misic sent the stern message: "To fall back is treason." The inspired Serbs faced the guns of the Bulgarians once again. This time, with the help of other Serbian divisions, the Drina Division held, and the Bulgarians retreated. The twin peaks of Kajmakcalan were Serbian soil, and the Serbians now occupied it. More battles took place before the Serbians reached their capital, Belgrade on November 1, 1918. In the fighting they lost 27,000 men or 1/5 of their total number.

Despite periods of low morale caused by malaria, desertions, lack of action in the early months, and internal disagreements between the Serbian government and Allied commanders, the Serbs were victorious, finally, after four bitter years of retreating and fighting.

The "Retreat to Victory" had come true.

A VETERAN RETURNS HOME
An Interview with Zlatan, a Teacher in Prizren,
as Translated by Branko Bosilkov, Guide and Interpreter

My guide and I were guests of a history teacher, Zlatan, in Prizren and were sipping the delicious strong black coffee sweetened with spoons of sugar, as the Serbian prefer, when a former friend of the teacher stopped by our table. Our host had started a story about some of the survivors from his home town who had been on the Retreat. After he and his friend heartily greeted each other with shouts and hugs, Zlatan changed stories. The new story was about his friend's grandfather, Miroslav Lukit, who lived in the same mountain town of our host and his forefathers. Here is the story.

In Zlatan's words: "A veteran, unshaven and wearing the ragged remnants of a Serbian uniform, stopped at the cafe where my grandfather and several friends were eating. The disheveled soldier greeted his friends with shouts of recognition and wrapped his arms around them. When they finally settled down, they had many questions for the veteran, Miroslav Lukit. He was believed to have died on the Retreat, but despite the incomparable hardships of his journey, he had survived. For some reason, word had not reached his village, even though World War I had ended several months ago."

Although Zlatan told Miroslav's story as best he remembered it, Miroslav's grandson interrupted frequently to add overlooked details.

"When the army began retreating in 1915, Miroslav and two other soldiers began walking toward the Albanian mountains in Montenegro, nearly 300 kilometers (more than 250 miles) away. They sometimes came upon fellow villagers, who shared their pitifully small supply of food. Unfortunately, his two companions died along the way. One froze to death, and the leg of the other friend had been smashed by a falling tree. With only crude medical care available, he died in great pain and infection. That left Miroslav walking alone for most of the journey.

"He told about his rescue from the Albanian coast by the French in Italian ships. He and hundreds of other soldiers were taken to the nearby Greek island of Corfu, where he recovered. Once he was healthy enough to undergo the daily physical training and instruction in the use of French weapons, he was sent with six regiments of other healthy Serbs to Salonika in Greece. From there, fighting along with the French and English, the Serbs were able to contribute their experience and valor to the defeat of the Bulgarians.

A typical example of a *"cheecha"* or older soldier who defended the rear of columns, a position almost guaranteed to be fatal. *Public Domain****.

Walking Home, Hungry and Barefoot

"Miroslav now was walking barefoot as his pigskin *opankis* had fallen apart long ago, like those of many soldiers. He had been wounded in the arm while fighting in Salonika in early 1918, but the English women doctors had helped the arm to heal. The plentiful food the hospital offered increased his strength, and when the war ended, he decided to start for his far away mountain home in Montenegro. However, by now because of his long journey, he had lost all his weight and strength. Toma, the grandfather, ordered a big plate of Miroslav's favorite food. They watched in amazement as he devoured the food like a starving dog.

"In the course of the fighting in Salonika campaign, Miroslav with other Serbian soldiers had climbed the great peak of the Kajmakcalan Mountain and fought at 8,000 feet above sea level. It was so cold and windy that the Italians who were stationed on the other side of the mountain had made no attempt to make this climb. Because of a shortage of mountain-trained men, Miroslav had been transferred to the Drina Division to use his lifelong knowledge of mountain climbing and fighting. The Serbians in the Drina Division set a record by their climb and subsequent capture of the mountain.

"With the war over, the traveler still wore his cap, a *sajkaca*, almost threadbare by now. Its distinctive shape had almost collapsed with wear. He was within a three-day walk of reaching his home near Lake Scutari. Miroslav was old enough to have been in the Third Ban, the oldest of the soldiers. Fortunately, despite his age, his health was rugged, and he survived the rigors of the Retreat. He told how lucky he was to have been spared from becoming one of the five thousand dead who had rocks tied around their bodies and were buried at the bottom of the graveyard in the Blue Sea. Many men from the same division, the Sumadija, had died who were much younger.

The visiting grandson offered to sing a song, and in a haunting voice, sang the same song of Serbians as they evacuated Nish (Nis):

Hear, ye brother Slavonians, A Serbian's mother's voice.
Enemies are rising, Our downfall to rejoice,
To soil by vandal force Our honor sanctified.
For liberty and Serbia, Oh, God, with us abide.
Come, oh come! Serbians arise, Follow, brothers, follow,
For home and family ties.

Serbia soldier, sick and desperate, wonders how he possibly can continue fighting. *Public Domain****.

The grandson finished his coffee and food and offered his thanks to us for listening to the story of Miroslav, his courageous grandfather. He bade us goodbye.

Our host, Zlatan, ended his telling of the story. We wondered if Miroslav had sent word to his family that he was alive and would soon be home. What would have been their reaction to his return "from the dead?" We would like to have wished his spunky grandfather, Miroslav, a safe "farewell."

We can imagine that The Soldier, sitting at a nearby table, would have smiled at the old soldier's grit. Miroslav would arrive home to the welcoming hugs and kisses of his family. They would pamper him for a few days, then set him to work in the fields with the one ox they had hidden from the army. It would be life as usual, The Soldier hoped.

Our historian friend ordered another pot of coffee with a platter of "knedle" (potato dumplings) and began another tale.

SOME BOYS GO TO SCOTLAND

Their number is unknown but perhaps as many as 20,000 young boys, aged 10 to 16, were conscripted to retreat to keep the boys from capture by the Austrian-Hungarian or German armies.

For many of the boys, the Retreat started out as an adventure. For others, this was their first separation from their family and was a wrenching experience. Few had been more than a few kilometers from their villages, so this departure generated feelings of excitement as well as fear.

The boys traveled in groups of 20 to 50, led by a few soldiers, or if they were not available, the village priest, schoolteacher or an important older citizen. For the adults assuming the responsibility for the boys, this was an awesome job, and tragedy usually occurred in almost every group. Their food, carefully packed in knapsacks by their mothers, ran out too quickly. Sometimes, groups of peasants roasting a dying oxen or pig would share it with the famished boys. Other times, the boys fell asleep with empty stomachs, exhausted by the walking.

One boy, seeing campfires of families scattered over the fields, compared the stars in the sky to the brightness of the fires. He found hope in a message that told him the boys were being watched over by each one's saint.

With this many boys, there were not enough adults to supervise the progress of the boys. They had to avoid the fragile ice covered cold river or they would slide into the depths of the water. The slick icy mountain trails caused many youths to fall and break a leg or arm. Some even fell to their death into the abyss formed by the steep mountains. There could be few successful rescues for this type of accident. The leaders often tied the boys together with extra shirts or belts or held on to long branches. This saved many from slipping on ice hidden beneath the snow.

The English medical teams that traveled with the peasants did their best to alleviate suffering and injuries, but the numbers of medics were too few, and the line of peasants and soldiers was often longer than the eye could see in the distance.

From the approximately 5000 boys who survived the Retreat, many were selected to be sent to England or France to be educated. No one remembers how they were chosen. Some boys were fatherless, some fathers had poor status jobs, while other fathers were wealthy merchants or priests. By whatever manner they were chosen, 27 boys went to Edinburgh, Scotland, where they studied and lived in the homes of generous Edinburgh families. They walked to the Heriot Boys School every day. The school had been founded 350 years ago by a rich gold merchant who served Queen Elizabeth I herself. The home was called a "hospital," the term used in those days for a school.

I was invited to visit and coincidently met some American Heriot relatives visiting there. I tried to imagine how the boys must have felt, most of them coming from small

Photo of ten of the boys who studied at George Heriot School. *Courtesy George Heriot School.*

Some boys were sent to George Heriot School in Edinburgh, Scotland, to live and continue their education. Each boy was assigned a number on a stone in the courtyard where he would report each morning. They lived with kindly families in the city. *Drawing by Vivian Kallmann.*

dusty brick thatched-roof cottages. What did they think about seeing this huge three-story-stone mansion surrounded with iron gates and gilded wrought iron fence? This was to be their new school. After school they went to their new homes with the host families. Records show that some became almost part of the family.

As for the other thousands of boys, we know most died. One particularly sad case involves the family of the Minister of Education who brought his 10-year-old son with him on the Retreat, hoping to save him. In the cold wintry environment, the child caught pneumonia and died. To the credit of the father, once he reached Corfu where the government was established, the minister continued in his job helping children of other families with their multitude of problems. We can only imagine his feelings of sadness, regret, perhaps even guilt, when visiting with a young boy—someone else's son.

Life in Scotland for Some Serbian Boys
A Story by the Author with Details Supplied by Mr. Frasher Simms

Bogdan turned to his friend Janko as they approached the huge stone gate. Its enormous stones were gray, darkened with black streaks from aging and covered with green vines. Beyond the gate the boys could see black iron fences, tall and topped with spikes like German helmets, except these spikes were black. Bogdan shivered at the thought. For an instant, he thought the Germans were in front of him. They were—in his imagination.

Janko put his arm around his slender friend. In encouraging words, he reminded Bogdan that those days were gone, that he needed to forget them. The boys were safe now with people who would take care of them. He understood some English, and the words the men spoke, along with their friendly smiles, convinced Janko of their good intentions.

The man at the head of the line, wearing the strange hat with a ball of yarn on top, spoke. He signaled, waving his hand. "That's good lads, come on in. This will be your new home for the next several years. You will like it." The other boys, 27 in all, looked at Janko to see if he understood what the man had said.

Janko nodded, and in his native Serbian language reassured the boys. The boys picked up their kits and followed the tall, red-haired man down a long path lined with square flagstones. These also had streaks of black but were hollowed out as if many feet had walked on them. The boys entered a large courtyard called a quadrangle. Tall buildings surrounded the quadrangle. The doorways were elaborately carved with words and dates.

The scene was unfamiliar to the boys. None of them had never seen anything this grand before. They stared in awe at the leaded window panes and the height of the buildings. Only one boy who had been in Vienna had seen such buildings. The village boys knew only straw thatched huts made from hand hewn trees. Even those who had been to Belgrade had never witnessed such splendid stone carvings. Belgrade had fine stone buildings but the blocks were square or rectangles and were devoid of words or figures.

Theirs Was to be a Life of Safety
A Story as Envisioned by the Author

Mr. Morris, the leader, lined the boys up so that each was standing on a stone carved with a number. "You, lad, are 147; next one, you are 148, and you are 149," until each boy stood on a stone with his number. "Now, this is much to remember, but each morning promptly at 9 o'clock, you are to stand on your stone. Then we will know if anyone is absent." Seeing the puzzled looks on the boys' faces, he paused while Janko hesitantly tried to translate. The boys smiled and each stood as tall as he could on his stone. Finally, each lad had something that was his and only his. They had shared food, even when they were hungry enough to have eaten several portions. They had borrowed or loaned clothing and blankets. Even shared water to drink or heat from the campfire. Now, each boy had something that was his alone—his own stone.

Photo by Nancy Cramer

THIS TABLET RECORDS THE EVER-
LASTING GRATITUDE OF THE TWENTY
SIX SERBIAN REFUGEE BOYS WHO
DURING THE GREAT WAR WERE FREELY
AND GENEROUSLY ADMITTED TO ALL
THE EDUCATIONAL PRIVILEGES OF THIS
ANCIENT & HONOURABLE FOUNDATION.
JULY 1919

Plaque presented to the school by some of the boys' families in 1919.

Mr. Morris read their names out and divided them into three groups. "These will be your classmates. We have used your ages to form the groups. Some of you may not have had as much schooling as the others, so we will change you to a different group if yours is too difficult. We want all of you to be where you can learn." Janko tried to translate, but he did not understand schooling based on age. In Serbia, a student went to school when he was not needed in the fields or pastures. Sometimes he would be much older than the others and would be trying to catch up. "Maybe that's what Mr. Morris is trying to say," he decided, and told the boys what he thought Mr. Morris meant.

Slobodan understood. Although he was the son of a merchant, and should have been in school, many times he went with his father to bring back the goods his father bought and helped to load them into the ox cart. Roads in most of Serbia, especially among the low hills, were so poor that only oxen were strong enough to pull a heavy wagon. But his father had died in the war at the battle of Mt. Cer, killed by the superb long range artillery of the Austrians. The Serbians defeated the Austrians in spite of the superior guns which were much better than the old Turkish Ottoman guns the Serbs used. The Russians and Allies had promised new guns, but…well, promises were just words.

Igor guessed at what Janko and Mr. Morris were saying. The son of a priest, he had learned to read some words in the Cryillic language the church used. He had learned by standing behind his father who read the words aloud, using a pointer on the page. His father had pronounced each word carefully so even the oldest parishioner could hear. Igor loved to read and even had begun learning Latin in 1912, when the first of the two Balkan Wars began. His father taught him, realizing what a good student Igor would make. Perhaps someday Igor would have studied at a university in Germany, where the great religious teachers and philosophers taught. But go to Germany, now? Impossible, they were the Serbs' enemy.

Mr. Morris pointed to one of the doors and said, "It's time for a bit of tea and cakes now. This is your first day so we will celebrate. Let's see what surprise Cook has for us." He led the way into a room lined with tables and benches. The boys sat down while older Scottish students poured tea into big mugs for them. The Serbian boys saw the pitchers of milk to pour into the tea, but they longed instead for some coffee which they usually drank with sugar. It had been so long since they had any sugar. Only a few times at the French hospitals had they been given some of the precious white sweet.

They bowed their heads as Mr. Morris motioned them to. He spoke some words so softly that Janko could not understand them. Afterwards, the boys crossed themselves in the Orthodox tradition and hungrily drank the tea and ate the cakes. No one could imagine what the next few years would bring them or what their schooling would be. Nor could they imagine the loving care of their host families and the teachers at George Heriot's School. Those days of fear and deprivation, witnessing the deaths of many friends and other travelers, were behind them now. The memories would stay with them for a lifetime, but they were not present today. The boys were being provided for and offered a chance to make a new life for themselves.

Safe From the War, But Worried---

This was the first day in 1916 when 27 Serbian boys were brought to George Heriot's School in Edinburgh, Scotland, as refugees from the Serbian/Austrian/ Bulgarian War which had begun in August 1914. The next year, the Austrians, bolstered by German guns and commanders, invaded again, and this time, their overwhelming numbers and superior artillery were too much for even the bravest Serb. Their army began a slow movement down the Morava Valley in the middle of Serbia. They might have been able to make a stand and defeat the two armies; however, Bulgaria chose then to attack from the east and form a pincer-like grip on the struggling Serbs. General Putnik made the difficult decision to retreat south, then cross over the Albanian mountains at three or four places to the shores of the Adriatic Sea.

The Bulgarians, because of hatred for the Serbs, were especially vicious in the atrocities they committed. When they learned that a few women had picked up rifles and joined in the battles beside their husbands, the Bulgarians hung dozens of women in retribution. They also hanged priests for no reason, including possibly the priest fathers of two of the boys who made it later to Scotland. Janko's mother was found to be among those with food hidden in the cellar, and as the Bulgarians were dragging her away, she showed them her infant daughter, still in the nursing stage. "My child, my baby will die with no mother's milk," she pleaded. The soldier released her and took the old grandmother instead. "No milk in you, old hag," he said and stabbed her with the bayonet he had removed earlier from his rifle.

All this Janko learned from his uncle who found him in the Drina Army encampment on the island of Corfu. This was months after they had made the Retreat. Janko never found out the fate of his baby sister. He wouldn't even let himself think of what may have happened to her. Perhaps sometime when he was grown, he would go back to their village and ask questions. That is, if anyone in the village had survived.

The 27 Serbian boys began their comfortable routine of walking to school from the different homes opened to them by the Scottish people. They attended classes together in small groups, learning Russian and Latin as well as how to speak and write English. They studied history and math, the latter in which some excelled because few English words were involved. Others studied geography, French, and German and enrolled in some classes of drawing and painting. One drew a cartoon on the back side of his sketch of a vase.

One boy withdrew in 1917 and returned to his home, perhaps in the mountains to help his mother. His father and older brothers were presumed to have died somewhere, perhaps on Vido, where the sickest soldiers had been hospitalized. Another student also left early.

Boys of all Ages and Backgrounds

The boys came from various parts of Serbia including Paljuvi, Kragujevac, Prokuplje, Sabac, Niksic, Ljuboviya, Pirot, Nis, Leskovac, Vranje, Smeredevo, and Cacak. Three came from Krusevac, but it is not known if they had previously been acquainted. None of them were brothers. The home towns of five are not recorded; one came from Winchester, England (probably had come earlier); and one was from Poltava, Ukraine.

Many of the boys went on to various universities in England and France, while the others later returned to Serbia. At least 15 stayed at George Heriot's until after the war and completed the 1918-1919 school term. While most of the boys made average grades, one student excelled in almost every subject with grades of 80's and 90's.

It was about this time that George Heriot School introduced sports to the curriculum. Rugby was especially popular, and two Serbian students were expert players. The Heriot team won many matches and trophies for their school. When the boys returned to Serbia, they tried to introduce the sport there with some initial success. However, in 1923 the last matches were played. Perhaps it was the competitive team sport, rugby, that brightened the days of the boys who must have been homesick occasionally. They probably worried about their families at home, and how they had survived the aftermath of the Retreat.

Of the 25 report cards retained in the archives of George Heriot's Hospital, as it was named then, at least eight of the boys had lost their fathers in the war. The occupations included merchants, teachers, priests, a rope maker, a manufacturer, chief commandant of the 30th Infantry Regiment, farmers, a police secretary, a lieutenant colonel, and a custom house officer. Higher ranking officers usually brought their sons along with them on the Retreat, if the boy was old and strong enough to withstand the perils of the journey.

Frasher Simm, the current archivist of George Heriot's School (as it was renamed), provided much of the day to day information about the Serbian boys. He shared the school's archives and allowed many photos to be made of them and the school. He related that other cities in England and Scotland also provided homes and schooling for Serbian children. George Heriot's School is proud of its Serbian students, as a way of keeping its original mission: to educate the "fatherless bairns."

The Serbian boys also were dressed in a traditional uniform of short pants, vest and jacket, and stiff collar with tie. They wore knee length socks, probably made of wool, and had the latest in English type haircuts, which was parted on one side.

Elsie Corbett's book, *"Red Cross in Serbia,"* 1964, contains these figures obtained from the Yugoslav Embassy in London:

"The Serbian Parliament was told in 1918 that at the beginning of the Retreat there were 27,143 Serbian soldiers and boys. Only 14,900 reached Bitolj (Monastir, in southern Serbia). The remaining 12,000 stayed in Serbia on account of sickness and exhaustion. The real losses occurred on the march from Monastir, crossing the mountains of Albania. Only 10,958 arrived at Tirana (in Albania), the losses being 3,952. At Bizerta, only 7,192 arrived, the losses being 1,808. Total loss on the march was 7,718 soldiers and boys, and to these must be added the refugees." (Courtesy of Louise Miller, writer and researcher, in Scotland.)

THE FUTURE LIVES OF SOME OF THE SERBIAN BOYS

Who were the 27 Serbian boys who arrived at Heriot School in August 1916 after making a miraculous escape from the German, Austrian, and Bulgarian armies in Serbia the year before? Other boys from the more than 5,000 who are estimated to have survived the major trek through snow and ice, up non-existing trails of tall Albanian mountains, with little food or water, were given second homes in other Scottish cities—Aberdeen, Glasgow, and Dundee. In a reunion in June 2016, relatives of 17 boys attended the ceremonies and programs. What the descendants had to say about their grandfathers' experiences at Heriot School may be summarized as follows: The boys acknowledged that Heriot School and the people of Edinburgh gave them a future to look to, when before, all they could think of was dying and death. For some boys, the "life preserver" was playing the unfamiliar game of rugby. They helped Heriot win championships, and on their return to Serbia, they set up the sport for other boys.

Stories Told by the Descendants

One boy, **Zivojin Kovacevic**, arrived in Edinburgh on November 1916, speaking not a word of English. However, he worked hard to become outstanding in both scholarship and rugby. He became an engineer and when he returned to Serbia, he helped with the reconstruction of the nation. Another young lad, Stevan Djorjdevic (who changed his last name to George) became a doctor, married a Scottish sweetheart, raised a family and served in World War II in the English army. He received the Order of the British Empire as a result.

Svetomir Marjanovic had been saved during the Retreat by the kindness of a important military chef, Spasoje Jovic, who even carried the boy on his back during the worst of the walking. Then, on Corfu, the man hid Svetomir from the doctors who separated the weak from the strong, sending the weak and sick to the island of Vido, where most of the Serbians died. Finally, a chance arose for Svetomir to join the group going to Scotland, and he joined the rugby team and "learned to be a good person." Those were the words of his grandson, speaking on behalf of his grandfather at a ceremony 100 years later at Heriot School.

Another boy, **Branislava Dulkanovic Skoko**, one of the youngest in his village, wanted to get more education. His parents enrolled him in a local school where in the winter of 1915 he saw Serbian soldiers retreating over the mountains of Montenegro. He decided to join the army and try to find his older brother, Peter Dulkanovic, but instead, he was sent to Scotland to school. He later received a Doctor of Medicine degree and returned to Serbia to study pulmonary diseases. He married and lived in Belgrade and participated in many civic affairs. He was most proud of his tie and pin from Heriot School as well as his Albanian Memorial Medal for crossing the mountains during the Great Retreat.

Another story told by a descendant of the original 27 boys was about his grandfather, **Zivojin Mirko**. When the family decided that Zivojin should go on the Retreat with an older friend who was a teacher, gold coins were sewn in the belt of his trousers by his sisters. Toward the end of the journey, the Albanians would accept only gold in exchange for food and lodging, so these coins perhaps saved his life. He lived with a Mrs. Tomory while attending Heriot School, went on to Edinburgh University, and became a construction engineer. His first job back in Serbia was to rebuild the bridge over the Rasina River in Krusevac, his hometown. (This was the town that saved itself by surrendering to the Germans.) Unfortunately, years later in 1999, the bridge was bombed and destroyed by the NATO Alliance.

Zivojin demonstrated his love for Scottish life by building his home in the architectural style of the Scots. Several of the boys also did this. He sang Scottish songs to his children and kept in close communication with his Serbian school friends.

The great-granddaughter of **Gavrilo Lazovic** spoke on his behalf. Her remarks were based on family stories as Gavrilo never spoke of the Retreat or life before it. He would only talk about his years in Scotland. When Gavrilo was 12, his father was transferred to Macedonia, and they lost contact with each other. This was immediately after the First Balkan War. Two years later in 1914, Gavrilo had the opportunity to join the Retreat. He was only 14 years old and fatherless, but nevertheless, somehow, he made it to the Adriatic Coast. This was part of what he never talked about to his family later.

But he eagerly shared his memories of his days in Edinburgh, the school, and the new friends he made. One of his duties in Edinburgh was to help an elderly disabled Scottish veteran of high rank, who later offered to adopt Gavrilo. But he badly wanted to return home to Macedonia, where life after the war was difficult. He wanted to go to a university, but his father's health worsened and he died. So Gavrilo took a job in the post office to support his family. He tried to interest his friends in playing rugby, but instead they chose football.

He married and had a family and was awarded a silver medal by King Aleksander for his work in setting up new post offices in several towns. He received other awards for his civic duties until World War II started. They had to move several times because he was in danger, and their house was destroyed. The great-granddaughter says: "Fortunately the 15-year-old boy who survived (the) Albanian Mountains (didn't) ceased to live in my Grandpa and he continue(d) to fight for the new life of his family. He was 15 then and I am 15 now…his great dream was to return to Edinburgh with the Serbian rugby team… and I hope that mine, as a…golf team (player)…will play on a famous St. Andrews Old Course…Wish me luck."

Another Herioter, **Dimitrije Dulkanovic**, was in his 80's when years later, he wrote, "We can never forget the hospitality and friendship which we felt everywhere in Scotland… we were homeless and parentless, so our gratitude to Scotland and (the) Scottish people will last till the end of our lives…" He was buried in 1995 in Zemun, Belgrade, wearing his Heriot's school tie.

Names of other students and a brief bit of information about them follows:

Djordje Aleksic-His father was a rope maker. Djordje's two little sisters lived in Vranje with relatives after their mother died during the Balkan Wars of 1912 and 1913. Djordje was 14 when he arrived at Heriot School in November 1916.

Petar Deretic-Was the son of a deceased Serbian Orthodox priest in Montenegro. Petar was 15 when he joined the group at Heriot School.

Danilo Djokic-Also the son of a deceased priest, he was from Kragujevac, the city which manufactured arms and ammunition. He was 16 in November 1916 when he became a student at Heriot.

Dimitrije Dulkanovic-Was the son of a merchant who had been killed in the war. Dimitrije, 16, came from Cuprija in central Serbia. He had two brothers in the Serbian Army. His mother and three young sisters remained in Cuprija.

Stanko Ilic-His father was a customs house official from Smederevo, a town on the Danube River east of Belgrade, and left a brother and sister at home. He was only 13 when he enrolled in Heriot School.

Zivko Zika Ilic-Was considered the most "musical and artistic of the group." He and three other Serbian Herioters attended the Tercentenary of the School in 1959 in Edinburgh.

Zivojin Kovacevic-Was 15 when he came to Heriot in the November 1916 group, and was the son of an engineer.

Milorad Maletic-Age 15, served in the Serbian Army but not in combat. His family suffered terribly from the war. His father was an army officer, his brother was taken prisoner, two uncles were killed in Albania and his mother and three sisters stayed behind in Serbia. Before the army service, his father had been a wood merchant from Sabac, a wealthy trading town along the Sava River in the northwest. It was the scene of heavy fighting and more importantly, the scene of a terrible massacre of the civilian population by the Hungarians in the Austrian-Hungarian Army.

Svetomir "Sveta" Marjanovic-Tall for his age of 15, he stood 5'3" and was "dark haired with even features." His grandfather served as Provost in Kucevo in northeast Servia and was from a prominent family.

Miodrag Martic-Age 13, Miodrag was the son of a farmer who enlisted in the army, leaving his wife and three daughters behind in Serbia. Miodrag was one of the youngest boys, when he joined the school.

Petar Milisavljevic-His father was a merchant from Knjazevac in eastern Serbia, near the Bulgarian border. Petar was one of the older boys, at age 17, when he came to Heriot's in the November 1916 group.

Bojidar Molerovic-Also was 17 and from Kragujevac. His records are missing. He attended the Tercentenary in 1959.

Djordje Nikolic-Attended the Tercentenary in 1959. His records also are missing.

Dusan Obradovic-Was the son of a lieutenant colonel and was 15 years old when he came to Scotland. He was one of three boys from Krusevac.

Djordje Osmanbegovic-Was the only one who could speak English when he arrived at Heriot's. His well-to-do merchant-shopkeeper family had sent him to Vienna for his education. His father was dead by the time he reached Scotland, and his mother remained behind in their home near Nis with her two small daughters. He reached Heriot's when he was 16.

Petar Pantelic-Despite his missing records, it is known that he was the son of a farmer who fought with the Serbian army and who was either killed or taken prisoner.

Danilo Pavlovic-Was 15 when he became a student at Heriot's. He was the son of a police secretary from Prokuplje in central Serbia.

Miodrag Pavlovic-Was 17 and the last boy to join the group at Heriot's in February 1919. His father was a chief commandant, 30th Regiment, Infantry, a high ranking officer. Before Miodrag came to Edinburgh, he had been educated in Belgrade and attended Cadet School in Poltava, Russia (now Ukraine).

Mihailo Radovanovic-Also from Sabac, Mihailo witnessed the shooting of his schoolteacher father alongside him by the Albanians during the Retreat. Remaining behind in Serbia was his widowed mother. He had two brothers, one became a prisoner of war and the other left law school to be a lieutenant in the Serbian army. Milailo was only 14 when he came to Scotland in the September 1916 group.

Aleksandar Savic-At age 16 he joined the November 1916 group and was the son of a merchant who lived in Krusevac.

Konstantin "Kokan" Stankovic-During the Retreat, at age 15, he joined a Serbian infantry regiment and fought the Bulgarians and Albanians. His father was a customs house officer from Pirot, near the Bulgarian border with Serbia. He was 16 when he arrived at Heriot's in the November 1916 class.

Milivoje Stefanovic-At age 15 he left his mother and three little brothers in their home in Nis. His father had been a railway official who joined the Serbian army. He came with the September 1916 class.

Toma Tomic-At 17 years of age, Toma was the tallest of the boys at 5'9" and a natural athlete. He was described as having a "military bearing and glossy black hair." His father was the provost of Leskovac in southern Serbia and also a manufacturer. Toma had served as an infantry soldier for six months before coming to Scotland. He had a brother who was a captain in the Serbian army and five sisters who resided in the home.

Miodrag Tutunovic-It was not until September 1918 when Miodrag, age 17, became a student at Heriot's. He transferred from a school in Winchester, England. He was born in Raska in central Serbia and had been studying in Belgrade when the war started.

Nikola Vasic-also one of the youngest boys, age 13, came from a shopkeeper's family in Ljibovija, on the remote western border of Bosnia which had been annexed by Austria-Hungary in 1908, with such disapproval by Serbia, that the Serbs almost went to war against Austria to regain the territory. Nikola at age 12 had fought along with his father during the Retreat. Left behind were his mother and five sisters.

Authors' Note: These stories, names and research were the work of Louise Miller, Edinburgh. She has written widely about the Retreat and Serbian war. She has also planned and conducted programs to celebrate the various anniversaries. There are some discrepancies in the list I was provided by Mrs. Miller and Mr. Simms. These may be due to boys being added or moving. Names missing in this story are Danilo Pavovic, Milan Djuric, and George Nikolic. Also, there may be misspellings of some names. The author apologizes for any or all errors.

GRANDPA CRIED WHEN TELLING HIS STORY
An Interview with Mile Milouahovic, Interpreted by Branko Bosilkov, Guide

"I was 9 years old when Grandpa died. He was 87 years old. I never forgot the stories he told about being in the Serbian Army in World War I. I never forgot how he cried with the memories of his escape across the Albanian mountains. It was a miracle that he stayed out of the hands of the German and Austrian-Hungarian armies chasing the Serbs. That was in the Winter of 1915. When Grandpa finally came home to his family at Koaxia, Serbia, he had served six years in the army."

The speaker, Mile Milouahovic, was a short stocky man whose smooth skin and pleasant smile made him look years younger than his 68 years. Only his slow movements betrayed his age. He spoke through a translator and waved his hands as he talked. Sometimes he shook his head and paused to wipe away his own tears. Grandpa's words were still running through his mind.

Mile continued, saying that his grandfather was born in 1868 but did not begin soldiering until he was in his early forties. He was the father of four children by then. Why he volunteered at his age to go into the First Balkan War in 1912, his family does not know. Then the Second Balkan War began in 1913. Grandpa fought in both wars. In 1914 Austria unexpectedly attacked Belgrade, Serbia's capital, and Grandpa was there to help defend the vulnerable city. Terrible as the fighting was, with Serbs outmatched three to one and overwhelmed by Austrian artillery, it was the nightmarish experiences of the Great Retreat that made Grandpa cry when recalling those memories.

The Serbs had only about 220,000 soldiers to call up, even after the government had conscripted every man of any age to take up arms. Grandpa recalled the battles were carefully

Mile Milouahovic tells his Grandfather's story of the Retreat. Mile is seated in the little mountain café he and his wife operate in the woods of Montenegro. *Photo by Nancy Cramer.*

planned by their leader, Voyoda Putnik, and they fought when they had the advantage of the land. Otherwise, Voyoda Putnik ordered them to retreat from the huge field guns of the enemy. It rained and rained, Mile said. The mud was up to their knees sometimes. The horses of the soldiers and the oxen pulling carts were always getting stuck. The rivers overflowed. Their native shoes, *opankis,* were always wet, and the leather thongs which held them together fell into pieces.

They marched as much as 400 miles southward through the Morava Valley. When they reached the Albanian mountains, they began to climb. By now it was snowing and the trails were icy and difficult to find. This is when Grandpa lost his toes to frostbite. He was without any shoes now, just rags covered his feet. They had run out of food several weeks before and faced starvation. Before they reached the mountains there was no wood to make a fire. Hundreds of men and animals froze to death.

Peasants and Boys Endured Same Terrible Conditions

The same conditions were true for all the peasants fleeing with the soldiers, and for the 20,000 young boys the soldiers had been ordered to commandeer from their homes.

Mile said the soldiers were told that on the other side of the Albanian mountains the Allies would be waiting with ships to carry everyone to safety. This rescue was all Grandpa could think of when he was hungry or tired. Once they started climbing the mountain, there would be few places to rest at night. They had to find an opening in the snow and all cling together, sharing what blankets they had. They had long ago lost most of the horses and oxen. Animals that survived would often lose their footing on the icy trails. The animal would then slide down the mountainside. They lay dead from falling or if they were injured, the people knew the animals would soon freeze to death. There was no way to rescue either animal or human who fell. Grandpa lost several of his comrades that way. He would later cry when thinking about how they had died. He had narrowly escaped death himself several times.

Despite a desperate shortage of food and ammunition, the soldiers stopped often to rebuff attacks from German General von Mackensen's four armies. At times the older Serbian soldiers *or cheechas*, few in number, fought rear guard actions to protect other retreating Serbian troops. Fleeing the enemy also were an estimated 30,000 peasants who left their villages and brought their animals along. Big sturdy oxen pulled hundreds of wooden carts loaded with the families' possessions. The food everyone had brought along lasted only a few weeks. By then, forage for the animals was becoming scarce, especially where rivers overflowed due to the continuous rainfall.

Scrounging for food was difficult, with so many mouths to feed. For the soldiers, at intervals the army's bread was brought in big wagons to them. A large loaf of bread was the only daily ration of food for the soldiers. There was none for the boys or the refugees. Added to the mass of people were up to 40,000 Austrian prisoners the Serbs had captured before the Retreat began. They could not leave the prisoners behind as they might harm villagers that remained. Other prisoners were afraid of being returned to their army because they had Serbian backgrounds. They chose to retreat rather than escape. The usual source of food was the carcass of an exhausted or dying animal that was shared by the hungry refugees.

As Mile Milouahovic related, "Grandpa told of being so hungry that when a horse died in its tracks, they would slit its throat to be sure it was dead; then eat the uncooked flesh. Soldiers searched the horse droppings for bits of undigested corn or grain. Grandpa's hands were cramped by the icy air, and for years after he couldn't make a fist. After he had been rescued and taken to the island of Corfu, he remembered seeing bodies of soldiers who died being taken out in boats, weighted with rocks, and dumped into the sea. The tiny nearby island of Vido, where the sick and diseased had been taken, had no more room for burials."

Soldiers Sent to Different Countries Survive

Rescued from Albanian shores, other soldiers boarded French ships that dodged German submarines to make the hazardous journeys to Tunisia or other countries. Mile is not sure where Grandpa was taken, but it was where he regained his strength and health. In a few months he was given a French uniform to wear. But his hat was the Serbian style. He learned to use the newest French weapons, and he and about 100,000 soldiers who had survived were sent to Salonika. Mile knows no more except that one day Grandpa showed up at their home in Kaoxia after the war ended in 1918. Grandpa would never talk about his experiences of fighting in the Salonika campaign against the Bulgarians.

He had been gone for six years. Mile said, "Grandpa almost didn't know his family any more. Life had been difficult for them the three years while the Germans occupied Serbia. There were killings, other atrocities, and starvation. All their crops and animals were taken to feed the German and Austrian soldiers. Mile told of how the Germans exercised a terrible retribution when a German soldier was killed. The Germans brought many trucks to the fields where people were working. They tried to run away but quickly the Germans rounded up 80 people and loaded them into the trucks. They were driven to where the German soldier had been shot. The peasants were executed at the same place."

Grandpa lived out his days farming at Kaoxia. His health was good. He didn't believe in washing his hands. "They would just get dirty again," Mile smiled as he recalled the words. No one ever argued with Grandpa; they felt so sorry for the violent nightmares and crying episodes he had. They were grateful he had been strong enough to survive.

"But one day, working in the field, he just dropped dead," Mile said sadly. "He had lived through the typhus and flu epidemics, fighting, and then the Retreat. But he died and was buried where he wanted to be buried, at his home at Kaoxia near the mountains. He was 87," he added.

(Author's notes: This story was told by Mile Milovahouio, grandson, age 68, at Kaoxia, a small mountain village about 10-12 miles from Divchibara in the central-southern Montenegro mountains on March 30, 2013. The site was a log house in the Montenegro National Park that served as Mile's home and as a restaurant. It was about 8 p.m. when we arrived, driving the winding road in the dark mountains. We were glad finally to see some house lights in the darkness. The restaurant had eight small tables covered with handmade table cloths, some with borders, some just cut with pinking shears. Mrs. Milovahouio said all she had left to serve were some huge buns, larger than saucers, filled with ground beef. They were delicious, but much too large to eat all of it. Their son and grandson came in while we were there and listened to Mile talk. The family seemed comfortable with each other. Mile had been a hunter all his life, killing wild game in the forests including, bear, deer, boar, small animals and birds. Presumably, they used some of the meat for the restaurant and probably sold some to local people.)

THE GRAVE OF A STRANGER
A Story as Envisioned by the Author

Dijana leaned over to trim the shaggy grass away from the frail wooden cross. Her back ached as she stood up to wipe the grass from the rusty shears. The faded black paint on the cross was peeling off. Soon the cross would become a mystery, just as the skeleton—the body—was. It was brought here several years ago. A man, Mitar Yankovic, from a nearby village laboriously had brought the body to her house where he thought would be the body's final resting place.

He told Dijana, "The caisson carrying seven soldiers from your village was pulled by two weakened oxen. The caisson slipped on ice covered by a new snow on the narrow mountain path. The oxen fell over the side, still hitched to the caisson. There had been no warning about the ice, so the men had no time to jump off the caisson," Mitar explained.

The caisson, oxen, and crew slid noiselessly down the mountain side, according to Mitar, who was with the troops following the wagon. Mitar was later stationed at the rescue encampment on the shores of the Adriatic Sea after the war ended. The whole scene had been eerie, they claimed, as no man or even the oxen made a cry for help as they tumbled helplessly into the gorge below. The bodies sank immediately into the ice covered stream where they stayed for months. After the war, and where there was no ice in the river, it was safe to venture into the stream, and the rescue of the bodies began.

Why had they not cried out? Some onlookers said because it happened too quickly. Others said the men were as exhausted and starved as the oxen whose sides were caved in from lack of food. Perhaps, others asserted, the men had long ago given up the will to live. The travelers following the group continued their journey, cautiously making their way along the narrow path. They hung on to twigs or branches growing out of the mountainside or made ropes from shirts for the children to hold on to. Others cut long dead branches to make chains to cling to.

Earlier in the Retreat, the refugees had sat comfortably atop piles of quilts and blankets in the wagon. The placid oxen plodded slowly carrying their great burdens. The bodies of the oxen were filled out from earlier eating plentiful grass and hay. Now the hay had long ago been devoured, and the grass was buried under feet of snow and ice. Now all except the youngest child or most disabled person walked along the path. Some wagons were abandoned, leaving priceless lifesaving goods behind. Everyone wrapped themselves in blankets against the cold. Such was the story Mitar told about the mountain crossing.

Besides telling about those who fell down the mountainside, he related stories about peasants and soldiers who injured themselves when they fell on the pass, breaking arms or legs. These injuries were bound with makeshift braces of sticks, belts, scarves or rags. Painfully they made their way to the tent hospitals the English medical teams had set up at the bottom of the mountain. Some people were unable to endure the pain. They screamed or cried or fell to the snowy ground, forcing their companions to silence them by a blow to the head. Tough as most Serbians were and used to physical suffering, there were some people whose toughness this time was not strong enough.

Dijana shook her head at her memories of Mitar's stories, wondering if her husband had gone through similar troubles as he walked to the welcoming Adriatic shores. Possibly not, if he was forced to take the fourth and most southern crossing. It was an extra 200 or more kilometers (120 miles). In that area there were few mountains, only low hills. His trials would have been of another nature, such as lack of food, fighting the Albanians with limited ammunition, fear, and mostly fatigue. She knew in her heart that he had made it to the safety of the Italian ships and then to the shores of Corfu Island. But her worries nagged her. Where was that precious letter from him saying he was safe on Corfu?

Yes, the grave looked better now. Soon there would be buttercups and primroses. She would let them grow, flowers for the dead, making the grave look less barren. The wooden cross was deteriorating and sagging because there had been no new wood to make it. There were only pieces they had taken from the small pen that fenced in the chickens. The chickens had long ago been gone. They fed some of the masses of Serbian soldiers that trudged down the dirt road of the village, looking for food. At first, a small child serving as a look out, warned her of the army's approach around the bends in the road. Then, seeing the soldiers' gaunt faces and hearing their pleas for food, she finally gave up, one by one, her precious egg laying hens. She cooked pots of rich chicken broth. The hollow-eyed soldiers gratefully drank the single bowlful she handed them from her cooking pot.

Now, she longed for a bowlful for herself, her back and legs aching, her fingers sore from handling the heavy iron shears. But she had used her last painkilling root long ago. It was not safe to roam the mountains looking for more herbs and roots with Austrian deserters hiding in the woods. She dared not ask the widow, Jelena, for some. The poor old woman probably needed a cup of the numbing tea every afternoon. Dijana still had here flannel piece hidden under the mattress, waiting to be warmed and applied to her back. Yes, that would do.

Questions for which She Needed the Answers

As she turned from the newly trimmed grave, she wondered where was the woman, wife of the body that Mitar had delivered, and who was she? Were there little ones? Mitar had brought the body to this village because the amulet the soldier wore around his neck was the one chosen by their village. It was also the couple's sign of love for each other and faith that he would return to her, the children, and their little cottage. There were no little ones now. The typhus had taken all three of their children. Their father had been unable to say goodbye. He was away somewhere fighting the Austrians or Germans. How could she be sure the body was her husband's? Mitar would not let her see the body clothed in its tattered Serbian uniform and wrapped in a winding cloth.

So, she accepted his word that the body was her man and buried him by the three little graves of her children. That thought gave her some comfort. They were all in Heaven now with the Holy Mother and Heavenly Father, who welcomed all the faithful. The unseen body in the grave, because he wore that special amulet, was surely one of the faithful. Her children were innocent in God's eyes and therefore accepted in heaven.

Her eyes filled with tears from the pain that existed in her heart. When would she could see her man again? Or, God have Mercy, she would someday hear of his death. Then she could turn the next page in her life. She, who never learned to read, knew a page had to be turned for another story to start. Another story—could she start life anew? Did she even want another story?

Crying now, desperate for an answer, she took one last look at the grave. The body of a stranger lay buried there. Perhaps his family, too, was waiting to turn another page and start another story. But who would tell them this story?

THE CHRONICLER
An Interview with Mr. Takoulevic as Interpreted by Branko Bosilkov; Guide

The gentleman smoothed his glossy silver hair as he approached our table. The briefcase in his hand hinted he was our appointment. He adjusted his fine silk lime green tie; the tiny tack pin of a gold bird denoted elegance and a source of financial ease. My interpreter asked, "Mr. Takoulevic?"

"Oh yes, indeed, you two must be the ones who were asking questions about Serbian soldiers who served in World War I. The dining room manager directed me to you. Now, what do you want to know?" All this was said in rapid Serbian, translated as quickly as Branko could.

Mr. Takoulevic sat down. We ordered coffees, and the waiter brought a tiny vial of a golden liquid. "My constitutional I take every morning, plum grappa," Mr. Takoulevic explained. "I didn't have a relative in the First World War, but I was born here in Pozega and my family has lived here ever since…" and he spread his arms wide as if to embrace the whole town. "Ever since the Romans settled the town in about 300 A.D. I have known everyone. I was the town mayor and officiated at many ceremonies. In fact, I am writing a chronicle about the town's history. It is to be a trilogy," and again, he gestured with his hands how big the trilogy will be.

"Cemeteries, though, that is what I can tell you about. I will show them to you and bring you stories for your book. Will that be satisfactory?" His piercing eyes looked at us, his aquiline, or perhaps Roman nose held majestically in the air. Before we could answer, he had lit another cigarette and placed it in the holder. I noticed several missing front teeth as he removed the holder with his nicotine stained fingers.

He downed the grappa in two gulps, finished his expresso and gathered up his materials at the same time. Mr. Takoulevic was a man of action. Off we walked to the nearby town center. Instead of the usual square, this center was a giant circle with short paths made of large square cut stones leading off like rays. In between the stone rays were smaller stones the color of soil, making an interesting contrast between the light colored large stones and the smaller ones.

A monument about 12 feet tall stood in the middle of another circle made of concrete. In the center of the monument was carved a broad bladed sword. Three words and the dates 1912-1918 were engraved on a sheathlike covering of the sword. A black chain attached to pier-like stands encircled the monument as if protecting it from intruders. The double headed eagle crest topped the stone.

"This monument is to all the people who died in the typhus epidemic of 1912. Doctors and nurses from England came and saved many people, although still many died. How many?" He shrugged, his well tailored jacket moved loosely across his thin shoulders. "Who knows?" he continued. "They took the bodies to the big pits and put lime on them as soon as they were dead. Perhaps someday I will write the number in my Chronicles."

(We learned later that this center had received a first place prize for the most successful architectural work of 2012. It was awarded by NIN, a weekly news magazine.)

He did not mention the famine that followed in 1913, another disaster for Serbia, as if the epidemic had not been savage enough. The village had had only 1,000 inhabitants before the epidemic. Perhaps they had stored enough food before the epidemic and it was sufficient for the depleted population. With the war of 1912, though brief, and death of farmers due to typhus, the food supply for the general population was scarce.

He announced that he had served as a director of a company also. Now retired, he is collecting photographs and information for his Chronicles. "The town," he proudly stated, "has 13,000 inhabitants. Quite an increase," and he smiled. "It is time to go to the cemeteries. Follow me, we will go in your car." He evidently knew the owners of all the parked cars by the hotel because he rapidly crossed the street and found our car.

We drove through rows of white stucco houses topped with traditional Serbian red tile roofs. The streets consisted of only two lanes, or just one lane if a car was parked in front of a house. Up and down several hills we went until in the distance we could see an old Serbian Orthodox church with two bell towers.

"The bells still ring. They were not taken during the war and melted down," the Chronicler boasted. The white painted bricks of the church were peeling; weeds grew among the flowers; and ubiquitous plastic bags and beer bottles littered one side of a small building. Next to the church was the cemetery, surrounded by a sagging wire fence.

Striding from one grave to another, his arms and hands always waving and gesturing, our Chronicler related stories for several graves. His stories were told, of course, in Serbian, and my interpreter had long ago given up trying to translate for me. I carried a small tape recorder, but again the Chronicler's rapid speech was too blurred to understand later when we played the tape. They might have been good stories, if somewhat disjointed. He tended to change subjects with the same rapidity that he spoke.

He pointed out the small chapel which had been built to honor the town's children who had died of typhus. The small church had a roofed walkway with arches made of aging brick. On the walkway about half a dozen headstones leaned against the church wall. Some stones were more than 150 years old. The writing was all in Cyrllic and weathered, although the stones were sheltered. Prominent citizens?

"The Chronicler", Mr. Stevan Takoulevic, told many stories about the war activities in his small town of Podega. *Photo by Nancy Cramer.*

Then it was time to return to the hotel. We ordered expressos again and the waiter brought the Chronicler his usual vial of grappa. Smiling, our guest explained that sometimes he needs two "constitutionals." At the time of the 1914 war, he reminded us again of the town's small population. Possibly, he had forgotten he had passed this important fact to us. "Here is my book for you, and thank you for yours. I like your dedication. I must go, my grandchildren are expecting me for dinner." With a flourish of handshaking, the Chronicler took his leave.

My interpreter and I looked at each other. Where was our World War 1 story the restaurant owner had assured us the Chronicler would tell? Had we missed it because he talked so rapidly and changed subjects, like leaves dropping off trees in the fall? Perhaps, perhaps the story was the Chronicler himself, an elderly and valued citizen the town prized. We smiled at each other and drove off to our next interview.

MY GRANDMOTHER, THE SMUGGLER

Interview with Slavisa Rakovic

(Not all the stories I heard were about the Retreat, but they told of what other Serbians did during those years 1914-1918 of the war. Here is one from a young man who was referred to me by his friend in the United States.)

My grandmother was a smuggler in World War I. It was unusual for women to engage in the highly dangerous business of smuggling. However, this plucky farm girl, Morosava Nikolic, seemed to thrive on risky activity. At the first call to meet the smugglers, Grandmother met in their secret meeting place, hoping to get a share of the contraband salt and cigarettes. The smugglers met their suppliers in the thick woods of the Novi Pazar of northern Kosovo, an area recently annexed by Serbia from Albania. The Albanians highly resented their new masters and were hostile, and the meetings always contained an element of danger for my grandmother.

Salt was expensive because the distribution was controlled by the Serbian government, and they placed a large tax on it. Cigarettes, due to the war, were almost impossible to buy. They were scarce even for the smugglers to find, and their value increased correspondingly. The salt was mined in Albania, packaged and brought to the border of Novi Pazar. The cigarettes may have been robbed from travelers or traded with the military. In the early part of the 1914 war, Albania was still a neutral country. My grandmother needed the money and was willing to risk being caught. She even chanced possible betrayal by one of the smugglers. In addition, she could have been reported by some of the local people of Kosovo, who had changed their loyalty from Albania to Serbia.

While engaging in her smuggling activities, she met her future husband, also a smuggler. After the war, they continued to engage in high risk activities helping the Belgrade Jewish population, although these activities were legal. In Belgrade, capital of Serbia, the Jews had achieved physical freedom from the ghetto-like conditions which had restricted where they lived and traveled. Now after the war, the Jews were not confined by the former limitations, they could live or travel anywhere. However, socially, they were not accepted into Belgrade's community as equals. Discrimination and ostracizing were still rampant in most social situations, sometimes subtly, but sometimes openly, resulting in fights, name calling and worse.

My grandparents considered it was their mission to help with the emancipation of the unfortunate Jews in many small ways. The Jewish community respected my grandparents for the rest of their lives. They were Serbs, standing against the opinions and actions of many other Serbs in Belgrade who still shunned the people of Moses. The qualities that made my grandparents good smugglers—courage, defiance of authority, and daring—also made them good humanitarians.

This story was told by their grandson, Slavisa Rakovic, who lives in Belgrade.

A VETERAN RETURNS HOME 40 YEARS LATER
Told by Father Aleksander Bugarin,
Priest of St. George Serbian Orthodox Church, Lenexa, KS

Stevan Bugarin was one of thousands of Serbian heritage who reluctantly wore the Austrian uniform when Austria declared war against Serbia on July 28, 1914. A resident of what was then southern Hungary, today known as Vojvodina, Serbia, the area was under Austrian-Hungarian rule. This meant he was forced to fight against his Slavic brothers in the Russian army. When the opportunity came, he willingly surrendered to the Russians. He survived the war and was held in Russia as a prisoner of war.

To his misfortune, the Bolsheviks (Red Russians) began a civil war with the army of the Czar of Russia (White Russians) in 1917. After four years, the civil war ended in victory for the Bolsheviks, or the Communist party. They immediately closed the borders to other countries, not allowing Stevan and others in his situation to return to their homes. So, for forty years, Stevan lived in what was called the Soviet Union. He worked on the Soviet farms called "collective farms" and was not allowed to leave the communes, even to visit nearby Russian cities. It was long and lonely life for Stevan without his Serbian family.

He stayed in Russia, married and had two sons. Back in Serbia, however, he had left a wife and a daughter, who had not heard of his fate and decided he had died. Communicating with relatives over that distance, especially if Stevan had little education, proved almost an unsurmountable problem in those days. Records show that about 79,000 Serbian soldiers were in similar circumstances and never returned to their villages.

However, Stevan, years later, managed to send a letter to someone in his old village, informing them he was alive and wanted to come back to the village of his birth. It was difficult to obtain permission to leave the Soviet Union, but he somehow obtained the proper papers and returned. Finally, with the help of the Russian village priest, Stevan received an invitation from Serbia for him to return. This paper was honored by the Soviets. In the 1950's Stevan finally arrived in his old home village, speaking Serbian with a Russian accent. The stories of his arrival and the status of his wife and family in Russia are lost now, Father Aleksander regrets. His grateful relatives bought him a small house where he lived out the rest of his life.

He told of the many hardships of living under the communist rule of the Bolsheviks. This is the story that Father Aleksander recalls hearing from his grandfather, who was a distant cousin to Stevan. The old soldier's heart always was with his Serbian people, and living in Russia could not change that. His Serbian wife, meantime, after some years without hearing from or about him, remarried. She possibly had died during the 40 years of separation from Stevan.

(I heard this story from Father Aleksander the week before my book went to the printer. Thus the story of Serbia continues to be told.)

THE CARETAKER'S STORY
With Interpretation by Branko Bosilikov, Guide

The elderly but spritely caretaker showed up minutes after we arrived at Zejtinlik, the huge 1914-1918 Allied Cemetery in Thessalonika, formerly known as Salonika, in Greece. "Want to see the whole cemetery or just the Serbian part?" he asked, his long white bushy eyebrows almost hiding his eyes.

"Just mostly the Serbian section, and we would like to hear some details and stories about some of the dead," my translator replied.

"To start with, there's about 30,000 soldiers buried here," he immediately said to my interpreter, who relayed the information to me. "It's one of the biggest in all Europe because the battles here in Salonika area were so fierce, especially the last breakthrough at Monastir and Dorian where the Bulgarians were separated from each other. The Serbs led that charge by climbing the twin peaks of Mt. Kajmakcalan. Buried here are 11,000 French soldiers, 8,000 Serbians, 9,000 Italians, and 2,000 English. But English soldiers are buried in other places, for a total of 7,000 English dead. There's also 400 Russians here and some civilians."

Our cemetery guide is pictured with another Srbian veteran who visited Zejtinik, the Allied Cemetery in Thessalonika Greece. *Photo by Nancy Cramer.*

He answered rapidly giving the figures as if he had done it every day of his life. And he probably has in his later years. That's because Georgi Minhalovic has tended the cemetery since his father, the former Keeper of the Holy Graves, died. The job traditionally goes from father to son, but that tradition will stop with Georgi. He has no son and laments the end of his family's role as caretaker. It is a prestigious position because it is awarded only to those families of a veteran who showed feats of courage as a soldier.

He straightened his army cap and shrugged his shoulders. "It'll be up to Belgrade to decide who'll take my place whenever I retire." When asked if he had any plans to retire soon, the question brought a fiesty response, "No, I'm only 87 and not even thinking of retiring." To prove his point, he quickly climbed the steep steps of the Serbian mausoleum and taking from his pocket a ring holding dozens of keys, he found the correct one. He opened the door, and we peered into the darkness. In front of us on the stone steps lay contributions and gifts from visitors. Georgi turned on a light, and an array of items in an orderly but crowded fashion met our eyes.

There was a pair of knitted woolen mittens lying among withered leaf wreaths, and several bottles of gruppa wine and glasses. The visitor is supposed to follow the traditional custom of a swallow of the sharp wine upon entering the mausoleum. Everywhere are fading photographs of faces in frames, large and small made of wood, metal or paper. Their gaze is sober. No smiles on these faces. War was serious business. Georgi pointed out a photo of one young uniformed fighter barely 15 years old. The lad looks calmly at us, his cadet cap at an angle. Old looking beyond the calendar years that he never reached in life.

Through my translator, Georgi tells about another student from eastern Serbia who left the classroom at 16. He volunteered when the Bulgarians in 1916 were getting close to the northern Greek border. This border formed the southern part of Serbia and the Serbian population, perhaps his own family, was in great danger from the Bulgarians. Georgi, with his eyes narrowed and a frown, told how throughout history, Bulgaria and Serbia had been enemies. Bulgaria's action therefore generated a raft of volunteers, especially among Serbs who had moved to America. They had become American citizens but they returned to Serbia to defend their other homeland.

Thousands of American Serbs Come to Fight

"A shipload of 400 new American citizens from Montenegro, Serbia's ally, sailed over to help. But unfortunately their ship as it approached Albania was blown up by the Germans in the Adriatic Sea." Georgi shook his head in pity. "These ex-Serbs and Montenegrians were inspired by the little publicized but heroic 400 mile Retreat of the Serbian Army in the winter of 1915 . The soldiers just barely stayed ahead of the German-Austrian armies through the center of Serbia. When they decided to cross over the terrible Albanian mountains is when the enemy stopped following. The way was too dangerous and costly in lives of men and animals."

Georgi added, "On the coast of Albania, Italian ships braved German and Austrian subs. French soldiers helped rescue the Retreat survivors. The French took the soldiers and civilians to safety in several French and Italian cities. With the help of English medical teams, many of the sick were treated on the Greek island of Corfu. The French also buried soldiers for whom rescue had been too late. After filling the small cemetery on Vido, a small nearby island, and Corfu, the French tied rocks on the bodies of dead Serbs. Their health was too far gone from starvation or disease. They filled small boats every day with dead bodies and dropped them in the sea. I'll never forget my father telling me about it," Georgi added. Again, he shook his head, his large eyebrows almost meeting as he grimaced.

Georgi started walking down the middle aisle of the mausoleum. Black engraved markings on each vault named its owner. Talking and pointing at the same time he explained, "Now this Captain First Class, he's from Macedonia where you (he pointed to the interpreter) are from." The portrait showed a mature man with a trim black mustache. His eyes and stern jaw a definite sign he was accustomed to commanding.

"This next captain," a portrait of a man with fuller mustache, lips clamped together looking straight into the camera, "is from Montenegro where me, my dad and grandfather all came from. My grandfather, Sava Mihailovic, was with the Volunteer Division. It was named that because they were all over military age but volunteered for duty. Sometimes the people called them *cheecha*. That means 'uncle.' They were assigned to the Russian army and fought the Austrians in eastern Europe, so he wasn't in the Retreat.

"This sergeant here," he pointed to a portrait hung in a corner. It showed a blond hair full face with typical Serbian cap called a *sajkaca*. "Well, he fought in World War I, survived the Retreat, and then got killed in World War II. Bad luck. We got a section here for those World War II veterans."

Mementos of Every Kind From Families

Georgi continued walking down the mausoleum main aisle pointing to a name here and there on a vault. He walked as rapidly as he talked. Answering a question, he said, "Sometimes no body was found, just bones. So we identified the soldier from the bones and uniforms and personal things. Then we brought the bones here to our ossuary." The caretaker's voice rattled and crackled. He rarely stopped for breath. Asked if there were any unidentified bones or bodies, he gruffly snorted, "No. We know all their names."

He moved from vault to vault and photo to photo, then started nimbly down the steep stairs to the altar. "Now down here is a picture of the lady soldier. You've hear of her? Flora Sandes? One day she just quit being a nurse, put on a soldier's uniform, cut her hair and picked up a rifle. She was a good shot, she was. Now here was Lady Katherine, but she was more than a nurse."

The double grave of the father and grandfather of the present "Keeper of the Holy Graves," Georgi Minhalovic, at the Zejtinlik Allied Cemetery in Thessalonika, Greece. *Photo by Nancy Cramer.*

(Note: Lady Katherine had been with the Scottish Women's Hospital but left to form the Girton and Newton nursing units of which she was commander.)

At age 63 she continued her work with the Serbs in such a worthy manner she was honored with this commendation in both Serbian and English on her tombstone:

"On your tomb instead of flowers
The gratitude of the Serbs
Shall blossom there
For your wonderful acts your name
Shall be known from generation to generation."

She died when a bomb hit her quarters at Monastir on March 7, 1917. Contrary to other stories that she died in battle, she was having tea with her daughters when the fatality occurred. She still has legendary status with the Serbian peoples.

We left the mausoleum and started toward the Crusader Cross that marks an English cemetery. Georgi asked, "Guess you want to see Lady Katherine's grave? English always do, so I guess an American would want to." Georgi took off over the gravel path that separated various parts of the cemetery.

There we saw the unusual grave of Lady Katherine with two crosses and the words engraved in both Serbian and English. Then we entered the chapel.

"No, there wasn't many other women in the Serbian Army. A few others, maybe." Asked about the women at the Scottish Women's Hospitals, his answer was, "They stayed at Corfu and in Serbia." We passed a dusty company guidon signed in ink by men of the company. Other flags and banners depicting saints embroidered on them were also signed. Some had victory battle streamers hanging down.

The chapel was filled with more remembrances, dried wreaths, homemade crucifixes and votive offering jars of various sizes and colors. Bottles of olive oil, candles, and little toys were left perhaps by children. "Can families bring things and leave them, or do they have to be approved ?" I asked. Georgi looked disapprovingly at me and answered emphatically in Serbian, "NO."

Portraits or photos had been attached to some vaults. On Vault 5568 a photo was posted with edges curling, showed a family at the original grave site. A tarnished brass plate had been placed on No. 5563 giving the full name, rank, division served, and village.

Copies and originals of certificates presented with the awarding of medals filled several glass cabinets. Rows of medals hung from the top. "Families give them to us for safe keeping," Georgi explained through my interpreter.

After walking us back from the British part of the cemetery to the small chapel nearby, Georgi reminded us he had other duties to perform. For his services he receives a small monthly pension from the Serbian government. We shook hands, exchanged names and addresses and thanked the Keeper of the Holy Graves. He cheerfully walked off, no limp or slowness in his gait. His hearing had been next to perfect, his skin unwrinkled, pink and smooth. He leaned over, straightened his regulation puttees, and then stood upright. He squared his shoulders as much as his slightly bent back would allow and off he marched.

We were filled with admiration for him and wondered at the secret of his good health and acceptance of his life, severe as it had been. Then we readied our minds for a walk among the many hundreds of grave markers waiting for us.

A WALK AMONG THE DEAD

The French section was first. The simple crosses had only the name, along with a symbol noting if the deceased was of Moroccan, Senegalese, Algerian origin or other than French but who had fought under the flag of France. There was no indication of rank or unit. The crosses were made of plain gray marble and stood in precise rows. Few flowers adorned the graves.

The British sector was easily identified by the tall slender black sword outlined with gold. It is called the Crusader's Sword and is mounted on a white marble pedastal. Installed at almost all the 2500 British cemeteries worldwide, it denotes World War I graves. A section to one side contained Jewish graves marked with the Star of David.

The British crosses had the usual elaborate, beautiful engraving of the crest of the unit. Each cross bore the name, rank, job, and unit of the deceased. There were row after row of privates who were runners in bicycle corps, drivers, sappers, or machine gunners. At the ends of the rows, the officers were buried, mostly second lieutenants, a sure assignment for a quick death. They had to lead the "over the top" charges carrying only a pistol. They often were among the first to be killed.

The usual custom of British cemeteries is to mix officers' graves among the enlisted men. In this cemetery there is a deviation from the practice. Mottos like "God's will be done" or "Gone but not forgotten" were commonly found carved on these crosses. Bible verses decorated a few already graceful stones. "Lovingly remembered by wife and children" along with words from "Nearer my God to Thee" were found on two stones. Some stones bore the crests of the Black Watch, a Scottish unit. For two years the British and French had been engaged in a frustrating battle with the Bulgarians along the Bulgarian border with Greece and Serbia. Some battalions lost 60-70% of their men in the critical fighting. The next year cemeteries were filled with men who died instead from influenza and pneumonia. Early in the war malaria had been the cause for much of the sickness. Rarely did a soldier die from malaria but instead suffered lifetime recurring episodes. Many had to be sent home because they were too weak to fight.

Scottish Units Lost 60-70% of Troops in Salonika

We counted the Scottish crosses. There were 17 second lieutenants, 11 lieutenants, 4 captains, 2 majors, 2 colonels, 1 staff nurse and 1 Royal Army Medical Nursing Service nun. Several RAF/RFC (Royal Air Force or Royal Flying Corps) pilots or observers are buried there as were 3 nurses and a sub lieutenant.

A large double burial plot encircled with flowers and topped by a large white cross marked the grave of Katherine Mary Harley, the woman Georgi had mentioned in a previous story. The plot was exactly as he had described it. Very large, yet plain and dignified. Two Russian soldiers were buried among the British units. The Russian stones have only their names and units engraved in Cryllic lettering. English flowers were tidily planted everywhere in between the stones, despite the coolness of the season. That was a typical English touch and is found at all English cemeteries.

The Serbian section was marked by the unusual shaped Orthodox crosses of white marble. White is most commonly used in nearly all Serbian military cemeteries, but in Serbia and Macedonia, the local civilian graves will feature huge black polished marble slabs and a headstone. Locally, black means mourning.

What do These Cemeteries Mean?

What does a huge cemetery like this mean to the loved ones of those who died and to us today? It is a beautiful memorial, but it also may be seen as an apology for a time when shameful deeds of carnage were committed. It also is a memorial to virtues, such as the tenacity and courage that were required of the Serbs. It is a time when an accounting needs to be made for the killing and suffering by both the soldier and the civilians. But how does one compute the price paid by the nine million men who lost their lives in World War I. These nine million soldiers come from all nations that participated. The number of civilian deaths range in estimates from 15 to 60 million, most of them from the influenza, other diseases and starvation.

Are these cemeteries built to honor the valor of the dead, or to expiate man's guilt at demanding the final cost? Perhaps it is some of both. Perhaps as many years pass, the value of life will outweigh the valor expended to protect life. We can at least imagine a time when cemeteries will be maintained only as a way to honor the lives of loved ones. Cemeteries will show respect for those who died in peaceful times. They did not have to die in a war. We can only hope.

Among the English buried in Zejtinik Cemetery are some nurses, including Nursing Sister Agnes Kerr Earl, who died after the war ended. Her death probably was caused by the many prevalent diseases then. *Photo by Nancy Cramer.*

ARE YOU MY GRANDPA?

A Story as Envisioned by the Author

"Papa's coming home! He was seen at the barn near the Kraloyevic house, riding an old mule." On hearing this, Josepha, the oldest daughter, began to issue orders to everyone. "Volsoso, go to the house and tell Mama and Grandma. We must all wash our

Grandpa arrives home after an absence of six years to find that he himself has changed, the family he left behind, has changed also. The baby he knew is now a small girl, who breaks the awkward silence that engulfs the family upon seeing the old man. *Drawing by Vivian Kallmann.*

faces and put on our best scarves and aprons," she commanded. She rushed through the sagging wooden gate to the tiny straw thatched cottage that was their home.

She stopped, dismayed at what she saw. Grandma was slowly rocking back and forth in the wicker chair where she sat most the time. Tears ran down the creases of her wrinkles. Were they tears of happiness or the usual tears she shed in her times of misery, Josepha worried. Who could know?

Mother looked confused and moved aimlessly, not knowing what to do. Could it really be her husband this time? She dared not to hope. She was glad that Josepha had taken charge. Josepha was ordering the wine glasses to be brought from where she had hidden them. She had done that just minutes before the Austrians destroyed anything of the slightest value in their barren cottage. Milos ran down the cellar steps to get the last bottle of rakjia they had been saving for this occasion.

Washed up as much as possible in their haste, the family members took their places by the front fence. Each hoped to be the first to see the man who was their papa as he came around the curve in the dusty path. A rocky overhang partially hid their view, and when the man finally appeared, he was so shaggy and ragged that he was unrecognizable.

It had been six long years since he departed to fight in the first Balkan War. At that time he was proudly dressed in the simple Serbian uniform, clean and well fitting, and wearing his proud thick moustache. Now, his clothes were filthy and torn, and his eyes were red and watery. His hair and beard had been uncut for months. Was this man really their papa and grandpa or just another homeless and hungry soldier?

They all stared at him when he pulled the mule to a halt at the fence. He made no effort to dismount but was silent. Tears covered his beard, making watery wisps of hair. What was there to say? And who would say it?

They looked at each other in helpless silence. He, in turn, saw two boys almost grown, his mother rocking in her chair, and his former plump wife, now gray haired with a thin, sallow face. And who was this little girl? There had been a baby when he left. Where were the other men of the family?

Everyone silently stared at the man on the mule, not daring to move or speak. Then the small child approached the unknown man on the mule. Innocently, she asked, "Are you my grandpa?"

Before he could answer, she asked again, "Are you papa and grandpa?" She reached up to take his hand and kiss it. He nodded and said, "Yes, I am papa and grandpa both, and I am home."

The Soldier, watching from a distance, smiled and turned away.

PART TEN

EPILOGUE & FINAL REFLECTIONS

THE CONSOLATION OF RELIGION, HOPE AND OTHER STORIES

Branislav Numic in 1915 penned a beautiful, inspiring missive that includes this excerpt:

"Motherland is not an object, limited, bordered and embodied. Motherland is an idea. Motherland is faith, and the idea of faith not to die; the idea and faith do not bend under the load of suffering; the idea and the faith do not fade in the darkness of forces; the idea and the faith do not disappear under the blows of violence.

We take a handful of the Serbian soil in our bosom, in the corner of a handkerchief. We will take our Motherland with us! Because of his deep faith, the Serbian soldier was able to endure injustice and hardships. He would look at the sky and ask for salvation and hope through prayer..."

How Serbian Children Fared on the Island of Corfu

More than 5,000 children disembarked on Corfu with the Serbian army. This included some girls as well as the boys, aged 12-17, who had been conscripted by the army. However, regrettably, this number was but one-fourth or one-fifth of the children who had begun the Retreat in Serbia. The exact numbers may never be known. Even after starting to receive medical care and the proper feeding, solid food was not allowed as it often ruptured the starved, shrunken intestines. More children died of exhaustion. After a few weeks of good care and gradually being allowed to resume a normal diet, the death rate dropped considerably. Those with the most serious health problems were transferred to the British Hospital in Corfu. For the rest, the concern was the future for these children. Corfu was too small for all of them to remain, and many of them were without any family members.

This is when the Allies stepped in again and offered to provide homes and schooling in their countries for these children, who were mostly orphans. More than 4,000 were transported by ship through the dangerous German submarine waters to Corsica. Many went to nearby Greece where special schools were established because of the language barrier, and others went to France and England to complete their education and be housed. In all, the young people attended a total of 43 schools and universities. Some had never before left the confines of their villages, and now they were exposed to a whole new world they could never have imagined.

Despite the multiple problems those countries were experiencing on the Western Front and the food shortages at home, the hearts of their citizens gladly welcomed the little lost children of Serbia.

For young men not healthy enough to rejoin the ranks of the army, the "Post and Telegraphe School" and the "Driver's School" were organized to further their training on Corfu.

Hope Overcomes Hardships

Many of the soldiers saved their sanity and preserved the will to continue by imagining. Imagining scenes of home, their family, the new baby, the old grandfather, the sagging fence, and the uncut weeds. They deliberately switched off mental scenes of fighting and dying, of friends being wounded, of relatives lying down, never to arise again. In one amazing book, *Sixth Day*, by Rastko Petrovic, a young boy walking through the ravines of Albania keeps one scene of a dream in his mind: "He was dreaming about doughnuts. Hot doughnuts. Nothing else, only about their smell, to feel their taste inside his mouth…" Those survivors, who were reaching their limit, began calling to their loved ones, words heard only by the other surviving fellow soldiers.

Then strangely, amid the safety and care the survivors received at Corfu, an amazing transformation occurred. After many men had given up any hope of living, they surprisingly began to show signs of life. "Hallucinations gave way to the beauty of reality." The soldiers now had food, water and shelter. But more importantly, they had a purpose again. Although many of their actions were motivated by revenge, other deeds answered the call to duty. For many of these soldiers, their motives also included their desire to bring peace and prosperity to families left behind to suffer in the enemies' hands. The survivors would, and could, be soldiers again for their King Petar and Voyoda Putnik. The Serbian miracle had happened.

A soldier probably buried where he died in a lonely woods. *Photo by Nancy Cramer.*

Serbian Metropolitan Bishop Dimitrije's Prediction

Added to his praise is the prediction of Serbian Metropolitan Bishop Dimitrije that "for our happier future generations, the island of Vido will become Serbian Jerusalem, a meeting place for grateful descendants."

The Environment of Salonika, Greece, Where Serbian Soldiers Were Sent in 1916

The Greek city of Salonika, now called Thessaloniki, is situated at the head of the Gulf of Salonika. It was a valuable port for transporting troops and supplies. However, the Greeks jealously guarded it from any unloading by the British and French in 1914 and 1915, creating all kinds of problems, especially in evacuating thousands of troops who became seriously ill due to the malaria epidemics in Salonika and had to be sent home to England and France to recover.

The city is surrounded by high mountains which overlook a coastal plain. Mt. Olympus to the southwest begins a chain of peaks running northward to the Serbian border. It was here that the experienced Serbian mountaineers provided the greatest assistance to the Allies, especially in the capture of the twin peaks of Kajmakcalan in Fall 1916. This opened the towns of Florina and Monistar in Serbia, but the Bulgarians made their capture costly in terms of time and troops. The British in the eastern part were assigned the capture of the Vardar River Valley, where the vital railroad lines were located.

The Child Who Was Abandoned and His Fate

A True Story

Ten-year-old Momcilo Gavric was abandoned in the early months of the war in 1914 with Austria-Hungary. It is not known what happened to his parents, but fortunately he was found by Serbian soldiers in the village of Trbusnica near Loznica. The soldiers, from the Drina Division, unofficially adopted him.

He even followed them in the treacherous crossing of the Albanian mountains, The soldiers sharing their meagre rations of food with him.

Once he arrived in Corfu, he became an unofficial member of the Drina Division and was promoted to the rank of corporal. He became the army's youngest non-commissioned or commissioned officer.

After the war, he was among the fortunate boys who were sent to Britain to continue his education. When he returned to Serbia as an adult, he held various positions and retired as a clerk. He died in 1993. (From the book, *Walking or Retreating to Korfu* by Ljubomir Saramandich, Curator of the Corfu Museum. Used with his permission.)

Praise From Foreign Leaders

Winston Churchill, British Lord of the Admiralty during World war I. later wrote in his book, *The Great War*, this statement: "The Serbians, seasoned, war-hardened men, inspired by the fiercest patriotism, the result of generations of torment and struggle, awaited undaunted whatever fate might bestow."

Commenting upon the courageous Retreat, **French Marshal Joseph Joffre** is quoted as saying: "In the circumstances in which it was undertaken, the horrors of the Retreat of our allies, the Serbs, surpasses anything that history has recorded so far."

How the Serbs Respected the English Nurses

Here are some examples of tombstones of nurses who died giving service to the Serbian soldiers. Their graves are in the Cemetery in Thessalonika, Greece. One stone reads:

NURSING SISTER
C.M.L. POPE
VOLUNTARY AND DETACHMENT 25TH JUNE, 1921, AGE 31
IN LOVING MEMORY. YOUNGEST DAUGHTER OF REV. W. LA. POPE BORN AT
REDBOURN VICARAGE HERTFORDSHIRE. NOV. 21ST 1889

Another stone tells about the Russian Red Cross coming to aid their Serbian brothers:

NURSE
M.C. RYLE
RUSSIAN RED CROSS
21ST FEBRUARY 1915
and
NURSING SISTER
P.G. SUTHERLAND
SCOTTISH WOMEN'S HOSPITAL
20TH SEPTEMBER, 1915 AGE 43

The Serbs Showed Respect for Their Fallen Brothers

Due to the widespread battles, especially small ones, the Serbs often buried their brothers where they died. (Some of the book's photos show these isolated graves.) But many small graveyards were established at first. Later, as the numbers grew, so did the graveyards. The bodies of civilians who died on the Retreat, were also buried of necessity where they died, in the fields or on mountain passes. In Corfu in 1916 more soldiers died from the Retreat. They are buried in 252 military graveyards in Corfu. Those who went to fight in Salonika, and were killed there, lie in Salonika cemeteries. It is estimated that the bodies of Serbian soldiers lie scattered in 17 countries as a result of being prisoners of war, or ethnic Serbian Austrians whose bodies were returned to villages in the former Austria-Hungary Empire.

Poem Honors Survivors

The Serbian poet, **Stanislav Vinaver** wrote this short poem honoring the survivors:

We endured, we lived through, We languished, we were resolute,
We upheld everyone's honor,
We glistened in battles, we drove away, we felt relief,
We began to shine like the sun, we overcame, we survived.

43 Allied Ships Rescued More Than 150,000 People From Jan. 29, 1916 to Feb. 19, 1916

This island was renamed by the Serbs as "The Island of Salvation"

I KNOW SERBIA NOW

My guide and I have traveled throughout Serbia seeing battle sites, memorials, and cemeteries. We've seen hideous stacks of skulls built by Bulgarians of defeated dead Serbian soldiers. We drove over primitive mountain roads where 100 years ago there were no roads. People retreated on slippery narrow icy paths.

What kind of people were these refugees? What type of soldier would continue to fight, outnumbered sometimes six to one, with artillery weapons at a 20 to one ratio? I looked at contemporary Serbian men as we drove through small villages and larger towns. Do these men have the fighting genes of their grandfathers? Do they have the courage and determination?

I found my answer the moment I entered the shaded gravesite of General Zivojin Misic, a few yards from his rural home. A slender wrought iron fence provided an island of respite for his grave with stalks of corn growing to its edge. A man born into a prosperous peasant family, and a soldier in three wars, General Misic, at times, doubted his own ability. Could he make the decisions that risked enormous losses of life or woundings? At times he disagreed with his superior, Voyoda Putnik, and voiced his disagreement. But

Bronze portrait of General Misic. *Public Domain. Photo by Nancy Cramer.*

he never deviated from his orders. The dark bronze bust crowning the gravestone showed his strength of character. His loyalty and ability were depicted aptly by the sculptor.

I realized that like the general, the Serbian soldier was a peasant, a man born of the earth and nourished by the land. He was fortified by his religious faith. His strength came from the soil he plowed and reaped. It dirtied his hands, clung to his clothing, and dusted his face.

As long as there are Serbs living on the land, there will always be a Serbian peasant. And there will always be a General Misic to lead them to victory.

A COMMENTARY ON NANCY CRAMER'S BOOK ON THE GREAT RETREAT OF THE SERBS IN 1915-1916

By Niel Johnson, Ph.D.

Beginning in 2012 Nancy, the author, visited Serbia three times. The last two trips she employed a guide-translator to take her to the places she had scheduled, and some that were not on her original schedule. About a third of the book is based on interviews with a variety of Serbian citizens, which distinguishes this book from other contemporary accounts about the Great Retreat of the Serbs in 1915-1916. The Serbs were trying to avoid surrendering to the invading Austrian-Hungarian, German, and Bulgarian forces. In 2014 the author traveled to Scotland to visit the school where a group of young Serbian boys were housed and educated after their rescue by Allied ships.

The author began this project by conducting a serious study of the history of Serbia. With that as a base and background, she has also drawn relevant information from textual and photo records. She introduced some fictional scenes and dialogue that are inspired by actual events and personalities recorded in other books, articles, and diaries by eyewitnesses.

These sources include accounts by English nurses and doctors, who accompanied the many thousands of Serbs, military and civilian, who were desperately trying to escape capture and probably severe mistreatment by their pursuers. Original writings by Serbian citizens are relatively scarce, reflecting the fact that the illiteracy rate in the country was about eighty percent. One might also note the degree of exhaustion and extreme environmental conditions experienced by those trudging toward the Adriatic Sea, over the mountains of Albania, to be rescued by British and French ships.

Courage and Tenacity of the Serbs

One thing that will strike the reader is the courage and tenacity displayed by the protagonists of this story. That can be explained in large part by the challenges that have marked the history of the Serbs since they accepted Christianity in the 9th century adopting the Eastern Orthodox church. By 1217 they had forged an independent kingdom. The kingdom reached its maximum extent in the following century. It began to decline after the Serbs were defeated by the Ottoman Turks in 1389, in Kossovo. In 1459 the Turks of the expanding Ottoman Empire annexed the country outright. The Turkish legions went on to capture Belgrade in 1521, which had been under Hungarian rule.

Meanwhile, the Croat and Slovene neighbors of the Serbs retained loyalty to the Roman Catholic Church, although they too, were under Turkish occupation for a century and a half after 1526. The Serbs remained unwilling subjects of harsh Turkish rule until the weakening of the Ottoman empire in the 18th century gave the Serbs new impetus to regain self-rule. They launched a successful uprising against the Ottoman Turks in 1817. Serbia had autonomy by 1829. But internal factional conflict delayed the process of gaining complete independence until the last Turkish troops left in 1867, followed by Serbia declaring war against Turkey.

Tensions after Settlement of War

In the resulting settlement at the Congress of Berlin in 1878, the signatories recognized the complete independence of the Serbs. Still, the Austrians were allowed to maintain troops in neighboring Bosnia and Herzegovina although these provinces were not officially annexed until 1908. Meanwhile, their populations remained mainly of Serb ethnicity. The Serbs also felt cheated out of territory they believed they deserved, leading to a losing war against Bulgaria in the mid-1880s. Tensions over borders remained, as did the desire to eliminate remnants of Turkish rule in the southern Balkans, and to redress the borders with Bulgaria.

The result was two Balkan wars in 1912 and 1913, with Bulgaria the main victor in the first war, but a loser in the second when neighboring countries joined against them and their expansionism. The Turks would lose territory, including land along the Adriatic Sea which became the new state of Albania. This blocked Serbia's hopes for gaining a sea port on the Adriatic. She remained land locked. The Serbs received additional territory, but this blockage of access to the Adriatic was motivated by Austria's opposition to Serbia becoming the nucleus of a southern Slav state or federation and thwarting Austria's own expansionist aims. Bulgaria would be forced to give up territory it had won against the Turks. That included land on which the Greeks had a claim. This defeat left a sour taste with the Bulgarians, helping to account for their joining with the Austrians and Germans in the subsequent invasion of Serbia.

"Powder Keg of Europe"

Little wonder that German Chancellor Bismarck, as early as the 1870s, referred to the Balkans as the "powder keg of Europe." Hoping to keep Germany from entanglements in the Balkans, he also said the Balkans were not worth the "bones of a Pomeranian grenadier." His sense of caution was ended in 1890 when the Kaiser replaced Bismarck with another chancellor who was agreeable to the desire of the Kaiser and his Junker cohorts to build a larger and more powerful empire. The complications of Balkan history, and the perceived need of the Serbs and her neighbors to maintain strong military forces, also shed light on an old Serbian saying: "Serbs are born to be soldiers." One cannot say that the Serbs were always the victims and not the aggressors.

Who Were the Serbs?

Most of the Serbs were also born to be agrarians, people who lived mainly on small farms they owned and who had primitive roads and little modern technology of the time. The nature of their life style also encouraged in them a sense of equality with their fellow citizens, and a suspicion of anyone putting on airs or acting like aristocrats. Pork, wine, and grapes were their main exports. There was not much emphasis on developing a system of higher education. The most literate class appears to have been the clergy—the Orthodox priests—and their institutions. The priests were among those most influential in inspiring the soldiers in time of war. The other professional and business classes, along with urban workers, had their roles, but they were not the kind of force to be found in the industrialized and urbanized societies of Germany, France, Austria, and Great Britain. As Slavs and Eastern Orthodox, the Serbs enjoyed reliable support and friendship from Russia, but Russia, too had problems in industrializing and educating its citizenry.

We may surmise that much of Serbian history revolved around rural communities and families who cherished their culture and took pride in resisting Turkish oppression. Those harsh measures only hardened the will of the Serbs for an independent state of their own. In the stories in this book, Nancy Cramer brings out much of this interdependence of the peasantry and their allegiance to one another. Whether literate or not, the Serbian families understood the challenges they had in common. They were not willing to leave fellow civilians or military personnel to the less than tender mercies of their vengeful invaders. Theirs was a common struggle, and one in which there was much shared sacrifice.

Witness the casualties left by war and also the ravages of a typhus epidemic. Losses amounted to about 370,000 or more out of a population of less than five million. As a percentage of the population, Serbia suffered more deaths during the war than did any other combatant nation. From July, 1914, when the country was first invaded, until the fall of 1918 when the Serbs reclaimed their country, the nation was constantly at war.

How Serbians Endured the War

The author makes such experiences personal with her use of facts from eyewitnesses, oral and written recollections. Her skilled storytelling engages the hearts and minds of the reader. War is not an abstraction. It is an experience that afflicts those involved with alternating feelings of pleasure and pain, success and failure, hope and despair, of courage and perhaps, of cowardice. It too often leaves the veteran with a sense of fear and terror that does not end with the termination of war. Such may be said also of the civilian involved in warlike conditions. These conflicting feelings often remain with many survivors as a post-traumatic stress disorder, although that condition was not diagnosed or even thought of, and certainly not treated, as it is beginning to be treated today.

So, we can only guess at how widespread the psychological wounds were among the survivors for years after the war. What we can appreciate is the willpower and faith in their cause these intrepid Serbian citizens displayed in resisting the tyranny of enemy occupation and temporary loss of their homeland.

Official medal given to the boys who survived as "Heroic Serbians" the terrible ordeal of the Retreat to Albania and to Corfu Island. *Public Domain.*

STRENGTH OF TWO ARMIES, AUGUST 1914:

TYPE	AUSTRIAN-HUNGARIAN	SERBIAN
Battalions	329	209
Batteries	143	122
Squadrons	51	44
Engineer companies	45	20
Field guns	756	558 (348 QF)
Machine guns	490	210
Total Combatants	**378,000**	**250,000**

Note: Montenegro, Serbian ally, fielded an army of 35-40,000 untrained men with only 14 modern quick firing field guns and some older pieces, models from 1870's and 62 machine guns.

(Source: Christopher Eger, Sept. 30, 2006 *The WWI Serbian Army of 1914.*)

Population of Austrian-Hungarian Empire was 56 million people while Serbia had only 4.7 million.

ESTIMATED DEATHS OF COMBATANTS IN SERBIAN WAR WITH CENTRAL POWERS

Serbia 98,000 killed or dead from disease or exhaustion; 115,000 wounded; 79,000 who never returned from captivity

French	35,454	**Austrian**	80,276**	**Russian**	3,180**	
British	23,762 (1,194 POWs) **	**Bulgarian**	246,019**			
Greek	26,000	**Germany**	84,303 (2334 POWs) **			
Turks	743 (180 POWs)	**Italian**	8,401-80,000 sick out of 143,000 deployed**			

* 1914-1918 ON LINE *International Encyclopedia of the First World War*, Mile Bjelajac, updated October 2015

** (Source: *Chronicle of First World War*, Volume II. Randal Gray with Christopher Argyle. New York: Facts on File, Inc. 1991.)

Exact numbers differ in various sources. Civilian deaths are quoted at 534,000 and were caused by disease, the Retreat, starvation, execution, and imprisonment. The typhus epidemic of 1915 was the cause of death of more than 350,000 civilians and soldiers. The death rate among soldiers was over 50%, not including volunteers from abroad. At its largest, the army numbered 712,005 men from Serbia alone. By spring of 1919, an estimated 3,300,000 Serbia inhabitants had survived the war.

ORDER OF BATTLE OF THE SERBIAN ARMY

FIRST ARMY - Gen. Petar Bojovic, Commander Chief of Staff: Col. Bozodar Terzic	
DIVISIONS	**REGIMENTS**
Calvary- Col. Branko Jovanovic	4 Calvary Regiments
Dimok Division Ist Ban: Gen. Vladimir Kondric, Comm.	2 of 13th Infantry; 14th, 15th
Timok Division II Ban	13th, 14th, 15th Inf. Reg. II Ban
Morava Division	1st, 2nd, 3rd, Inf. Reg. II Ban
Branicevo detachment (Dunav Division II Ban)	7th, 8th, 9th Inf. Reg II Ban, Other troops: 9th Inf. Reg. I Ban, and 8th, and 9th Inf. Reg III Ban
Army Artillery	Col. Bozidar Sreckovic

SECOND ARMY - Gen. Stepa Stepanovic, Commander Chief of Staff: Col. Vojislav Zivanovic	
DIVISIONS	**REGIMENTS**
Morava Division I Ban: Col. Ilija Gojkovic	1st, 2nd, 3rd Inf. Reg. I Ban, 16th Inf. Reg. I Ban
Combined Division I Ban: Gen. Mihajlo Rasic	1st, 2nd, 5th Svetislav Miskovic *Supernumerary Inf. Reg. I Ban, 6th supernumerary Inf. Reg. I Ban Dragoljub Uzunmirkovic
Sumadija I Ban	10th, 11th, 12th, 19th Inf. Reg I Ban
Dunav Division I Ban- Milivoje Andelkovic	7th, 8th, 18th Inf. Reg I Ban, 4th Supernumerary Inf. reg 1st Ban
Army Artillery	

THIRD ARMY - Gen. Pavle Jurisic Strum, Commander Chief of Staff: Col. Dusan Pesic	
DIVISON AND BRIGADES	**REGIMENTS**
Drina Division I Ban	5th, 6th, 17th Inf. Reg I Ban, 3rd Supernumerary Inf. Reg. I Ban
Drina Division II Ban	5th Inf. Reg II Ban, Miloje Jelisijevic, 1st Batt. of 5th Inf. Reg III Ban
Obrenovac Detachment	7th Inf. Reg III Ban, 2nd Batt of 5th Inf. Reg III Ban, Jadar Cetnik Detachment

OTHER UNITS	
ARMY ARTILLERY - Col. Milos Mihailovic	
ARMY GROUP UZICE - Gen. Milos Bozanvic	
DIVISONS AND BRIGADES	**REGIMENTS**
Sumadija Divison II Ban- Col. Dragutin Milutinovic	10th, 11th, 12th, Inf. Reg II Ban, 4th Inf. Reg. 1st Ban
Uzice Brigade- Col. Ivan Pavlovic	4th Inf. Reg II Ban; 4th Inf. Reg II Ban
Detachments:	Lim Detach.- Lt. Col Jevrem Mihailovic, Zlatibor Cet** Detach.-Maj. Kosta, Tododrovic; Gornjak Cetnik Deta Maj. Velimir Vemic
Army Artillery	
*Supernumerary: means troops not counted as regular army units ** Chetniks are guerillas	

FREEDOM FIGHTERS FROM KANSAS CITY, MISSOURI AREA JOIN SERBIAN FORCES

In the Summer of 1915, 19 men from the Kansas City, MO area sailed to Europe to fight for the freedom of Serbia. They were among the 5,000 Serb-Americans who joined their beleaguered Serbian brothers.

Their names are: Jovo Pokrajac, Ilija Skorupan (killed in action), Jovo Krajnovic, Manr Vukas, Janko Jovic, Petar Zuzic, Mile Grba Marko Ogrizovic, Dusan Dragicevic, Vajo Vlasic, Marko Podkonjak, Stevan Pocuca, Ilija Kalinic, Mile Dragas, Iso Jovic, Jovan Uzelac, Luka Phualo, and Dmitar Obradovic.

Only three returned to Kansas City. One was Luka Pahalo who received a citation for his heroism by King Petar. Two, Jovan Uzelac and Dmitar Obradovic, later moved to California.

All the men were members of the local chapter of the Pan-Slavic youth organization called "Sokoli" or "Falcons." Two men, Mirko Vukas and Nikola Licina, and other Serbs served in the American army during 1917 -1918. The story does not stop here. In 1917 a second group of Freedom Fighters went to Serbia to fight for their Motherland. Among them were these names which have been recorded: Djuro Grkovic, Illije Jovetic, Grba Gajo Grba, Mane Jovetic, Dragan Supica, Petar Ninkovic, Simo Sumonja,and Stevan Jovic. (*This information was supplied by Father Aleksander Bugarin, priest of the St. George Serbian Orthodox Church, Lenexa, Kansas.*)

GRAVEYARDS, COMMEMORATIONS, MONUMENTS AND SACRAMENT

The Serbian military graveyards denote the sacrifice that Serbia made during her struggle for freedom and existance at the time of the First World War. The scattered Serbs in exile left their bones in 17 countries.

From 1916-1918, while fighting in the territory of Greece, the Serbian army founded 252 military graveyards on the island of Corfu, in Salonika and at the Salonika front. The largest Serbian military graveyard was the one in Salonika with 7,444 graves.

On the Island of Corfu 28 military graveyards were founded. The largest ones were with the division camps: Gouvia, South Ipsos, North Ipsos, Strongili, Mesonghi, Aghios Mattheos, Vraganiotiki and Katomeri. The largest among them were the graveyards near the village Katomeri with 560 and Aghios Mattheos with 520 graves.

The officers graveyard was around the Achillion Palace. The refugees were buried at the city graveyard Garitsa and at Village graveyards.

(Spelling and wording as copied from a plaque.)

BIBLIOGRAPHY
for *"Retreat to Victory"*

Adams, John Clinton. *Flight in Winter "But pray that your flight be not in winter."* Matthew 24:20. Princeton: Princeton, NJ. University Press. 1942.

Aldridge, Alice. *The Retreat from Serbia through Montenegro and Albania.* Reprint of University of Michigan Library, Ann Arbor, MI. 1916.

Bailey, W. F., *The Slavs of the War Zone.* London: Chapman & Hall, 1917.

Bjelajac, Mile. 1914-1918 ON LINE. *International Encyclopedia of the First World War.* Updated 01 October 2015.

Colinson, Owen. *Salonica and after.* (A critique of the way the war was fought there with needless loss of life due to malaria and other illnesses.) 1919.

Corbett, Elsie. *The Red Cross in Serbia: A personal Diary of Experience, 1915- 1919.* Publisher unknown.

Di Nardo, Richard L. *Invasion. The Conquest of Serbia. 1915.* Santa Barbara, CA: Praeger. 2015.

Gerolymatos, Andre. *The Balkan Wars. Conquest, Revolution and Retribution From Ottoman Era to the Twentieth Century and Beyond.* New York: Basic Books, 2002.

Glenny, Misha. *The Balkans. Nationalism, War, and the Great Powers, 1804-2011.* New York: Penguin Books, 2012.

Gordon, Gordon-Smith. *Through the Serbian Campaign Plan.* Reprint of University of Michigan Library, Ann Arbor, Michigan. 1916. (English correspondent travels with the Retreat.)

———*From Serbia to Jugoslavia.* New York: G.P. Putnam's Sons. 1920.

Gray, Randall and Argyle, Christopher. *Chronicle of First World War, Vol. II* New York: Facts on File. 1991.

Hupchick, Dennis P. and Cox, Harold. *The Palgrave Concise Historical Atlas of the Balkans.* New York: Palgrave, 2001.

Jones, Fortier. *With Serbia into Exile, An American's adventures with the Army that Cannot Die.* Reprint of Cornell University, 1916.

Judah, Tim. *The Serbs. History, Myth, and Destruction of Yugoslavia.* 3rd Ed. New Haven and London: Yale University. 2009.

Kaplan, Robert. *Balkan Ghosts*. New York: St. Martin's Press. 1993.

Mazower, Mark. *The Balkans. A Short History*. New York: Modern Library. 2002

McLaren, Eva Shaw. *A History of the Scottish Women's Hospitals*. Memphis, Tenn. 2012.

Mitrovic, Andrej. *Serbia's Great War 1914-1918*. London: C. Hurst & Co. Ltd. 2007.

Owen, Collinson. *Balkan Victory*. London. Hoddon and Stoughton. 1919.
    Reprint by Forgotten Books, 2012.

———*Salonica and After: The Sideshow That Ended the War*. London: Hodder and
    Stoughton, 1919. First published. 2nd publishing by Forgotten Books. 2012.
    (English correspondent during the war)

Palmer, Alan. *The Gardeners of Salonika*. New York: Simon and Schuster. 1965.

Ross, Ishobel. *Little Grey Partridge*. Aberdeen, U.K.: Aberdeen University Press. 1988.
    (True story of young English nurse's experiences in Salonika.)

Saramandic, Ljubomir. *Walking or Retreating to Corfu* published in Serbia. (Can be
    obtained by writing the Curator of Corfu Museum, for an English translation.

Schevill, Frederick. *History of the Balkan Peninsula*. New York: Frederick Ungar Publ.
    Co. 1922. Republished in 1966 from the estate.

Snyder, Louis L. *Historic Documents of World War I*. Princeton, N.J.: Von Nostrand
    Co., Inc. 1958.

Stebbing, E.P. *At the Serbian Front in Macedonia*. London: John Lane, The Bodley
    Head. 1917.

Stevens, Stevan Idjidovic. *The Snows of Serbia. A Child Soldier in the Great War*. 2012.
    No publisher listed.

Stobart, Mabel Annie. *The Flaming Sword in Serbia and Elsewhere*. Reprint of Miami,
    FL: Hard Press Publ. (originally published by Hodder and Stoughton, London
    in 1917. This woman spearheaded worldwide medical aid and other help for the
    Serbs, then later, she worked in other countries.

Strachan, Hew. *The First World War*. New York: Penguin Books. 2003.

West, Rebecca. *Black Lamb and Grey Falcon. A Journey Through Yugoslavia*. London:
    MacMillan Press. 1942.

Winchester, Simon. *The Fracture Zone. A Return to the Balkans*. New York: Harper
    Collins. 1999. (One of many excellent books about the crises in The Balkans in
    the 1990's.)

ABOUT THE ARTIST

The artist, Vivian Nast Kallman Faulkner, was born in New York City, where she started drawing at the Arts Student's League at age 12. Her work concentrated mostly on leaded and stained glass, fulfilling private commissions across the United States. She now works in other mediums including portraits, free form in pen and ink, architectural renderings, landscapes, water color, oil, and even stone. She was the creator of the drawings in Ms. Cramer's children's book, *Beko, the Little French Dog*.

ABOUT THE AUTHOR

Nancy Cramer

I taught both elementary school children and adults for nearly 30 years, and had a parttime private practice as a Licensed Professional Counselor for nearly 20 years. I judged the Greater Kansas City Science Fair for almost 35 years, and also oratorical contests. In addition, I served in leadership roles for nearly 30 years with the Missouri National Education Association.

I began writing in 2007 after I sold the fire suppression business that I inherited when my husband died in 1994. Finally, I had time to write. This book is the fifth book about World War I, and I was inspired by my volunteering these past seven year at the world famous National World War I Museum and Memorial in Kansas City. I have served on the Advisory Board of the Bellefontaine Corps Salvation Army for 22 years and take pleasure in bell ringing each Christmas. As you can see I enjoy living and learning.

The author, Nancy Cramer

ABOUT THE ASSISTANT EDITOR

Niel Johnson, Ph.D., retired in December 1992, after serving 15 years as an archivist and oral historian with the Truman Library in Independence, MO. Previously, he taught history at the college level and authored several books, including *George Sylvester Viereck: German-American Propagandist* (Univ. of Ill. Press. 1972) and *Power, Money, and Women: Words to the Wise from Harry S. Truman,* as well as articles for history journals. For six years, he also was the historian of the headquarters, Army Weapons Command, and Rock Island Arsenal. He is best known since 1993 as an impersonator of President Harry S. Truman and has played that role in various parts of the United States. He received his doctorate in American history from the State University of Iowa.

A Letter of Gratitude From Serbian Boys

42. Blacket-Place,
Edinburgh.
20th January 1917.

Dear Sir Robert,

On behalf of the Serbian Boys I wish to let you know that we all enjoyed ourselves very much last Saturday afternoon at the Tea and Concert at George Heriots School. We all liked the music very much and were pleased to think that the Scottish people enjoyed the Serbian national songs. We all wish to thank you also for the nice lines of poetry you sent us and hope to benefit from the good advice contained in them

I am,
Yours Sincerely,
Djordje Osmanbegović.

Milivoye Stefanovitch.
Milorag Maletich.
Demitri Dulkanovitch.
Djordje Aleksitch.
Peter Pantelitch
Mihailo Radovanovitch.
Nikola Vasitch
Stanko Ilitch.
Miodrag Martitch
Miivo Mitch
Danilo Pavlovitch.

Yanik Lazmich
Dushan Obradovitch.
George Nikolitch.
Svetomir Marganovitch.
Toma Tomitch.
Konstantin Standovitch
Alexander Savitch
Bahilov Milyaoitch.
Steo Iestitch
Zivojin
Danilo Djokitch.
Peter Milisavlyovitch
Milan Djuritch.

Serbians dance traditional Kola around a cairn of stones carrying the names of their victories. *Public Domain****.

Serbian soldier wrapped in blankets guards supply wagons near Albanian border. *Public domain****.

Medal awarded to the soldier survivors of the retreat. It is a tri-colored ribbon, (left to right) red, blue and white and approximately two inches long. *Public Domain.*